THE WIND BLEW AND THE SHIP FLEW

WILLIAM ERNEST MERYMAN

Second edition © 2016 Coastlore Media. All rights reserved.
PO Box 8491, Portsmouth, New Hampshire 03802-8491

First edition ©1982, William Ernest Meryman

Contents

Introduction to the 2016 edition   Page 6

Foreword   7

Chapter 1	**THE TALL SHIPS** The rise and fall of American clipper ships.	8
Chapter 2	**THE IRON MEN** Clipper and packet ship captains, and their Maine counterparts.	17
Chapter 3	**TWO TOWNS IN MAINE** Brunswick and Harpswell, birthplace of shipbuilders and seafarers.	25
Chapter 4	**BUILDING THE SHIP** American sailing ship building—how, when, and where.	33
Chapter 5	**THE FLIP SIDE** Maritime disasters—the sad fate of some Brunswick-Harpswell ships.	42
Chapter 6	**THE COASTAL CLANS** Shipbuilding families and their captains.	49
Chapter 7	**CAPT. JACOB AND CAPT. SAM** Two different types of successful shipmasters.	56
Chapter 8	**THE TEAM ROSTER** Brief sketches of representative Maine sea captains.	66
Chapter 9	**THE LADIES, BLESS 'EM** The contributions of women to Maine's "glory era" of sail.	75
Chapter 10	**AFTER THE FACT** A summation, update, and a personal assessment.	83

INTRODUCTION TO THE 2016 EDITION

William Ernest Meryman (1916-1994)—known early in life as "Ernie" and later as "Bill"—was my stepfather. He lived most of his life near Boston in the coastal suburbs of Winthrop and Lynn. He had an abiding pride and passion regarding his legacy as the son of a Boston Harbor lobsterman and the descendant of shipbuilders and sea captains in Maine.

That passion led him to write this book, which he first published in 1982. He wrote the original manuscript in longhand and my mother, Beatrice Meryman, dutifully typed it. In this new edition I've corrected a few stray typos, but the text is at least 99% as it was originally written.

Bill was never a professional writer, but he was highly intelligent and very well read. Deep in his soul, Bill was a poet with an affinity for the sea. Many of his poems appeared over the years in his hometown newspaper, the *Winthrop Sun Transcript*, and some of them are sprinkled in the pages of this book.

Republishing this book is a way of saying thank you to Bill Meryman, whose passion for the sea, ships, and sailors had an enormous influence on my life. I hope you enjoy it.

Jeremy D'Entremont
Portsmouth, NH
January 2016

FOREWORD

It is doubtful that anything ever created by man has equaled, in beauty and pure majesty, the great clipper ships of the mid-1800s. Their emotional impact upon us has never been log although they have been gone for a hundred years or more. Their story is recounted here as a fitting prelude to the true tale of the sailing ship era in one small section of the Maine coast.

For nearly a century, the building of wooden ships along the coast of Maine was a flourishing business. Shipyards were strung out along its jagged shoreline and larger rivers in great number and Casco Bay towns in particular were almost literally bursting with activity. Brunswick and Harpswell were near the center of this open ring, which extended from Cape Elizabeth to Portland and northeastward to the river towns of Bath, Wiscasset, and Damariscotta. Shipbuilding in Portland and Bath has been well recorded, and Bath continues to be a major builder of modern vessels for the U.S. Navy. Not as well known is the short but highly concentrated story of Brunswick and Harpswell.

But this is more than a sketchy history of the sailing ships and their captains. The lives of the coastal dwellers themselves were equally colorful and important. My own family was but one many who were involved in Harpswell's day in the sun, and I have made a particular effort not to overstate the role they played in the picture of their time.

Research for this work included many reliable sources, mainly private. Principal contributors are credited in the text. I am grateful, too, for the skilled assistance of my wife, Beatrice, whose appreciation of true beauty has always included sailing ships and the sea.

My family left Maine well over a century ago, as did man others in that period. Today their descendants are scattered all over this country. Perhaps we can never "go home again," but for most of us Maine still holds a special place in our lives wherever we happen to be today.

W. E. Meryman
Lynn, Massachusetts
1982

I
THE TALL SHIPS

She was more than a man could resist, full bosomed and free on the ocean sea, graceful and proud, awesomely grand. She was all of that, and more. Literally the goddess of the sea she was, a superior class of sailing ship numbering into the hundreds, sparkling upon the oceans of the world for an all too brief span of years around the middle of the nineteenth century. Yet the Yankee clippers remain today, more than a hundred years since the close of their meteoric careers, the living symbols of high adventure to anyone fancying a dash of salt water in his veins. They were an emotional experience without equal to most people fortunate enough to have seen them, much less serve aboard them at sea.

Today, although we can only envy that experience, we somehow feel that we understand how it was for those outrageously lucky people, living at that time in or around the ports of the world. The very names of these high bred ladies of the sea stir our imaginations still — the *Flying Cloud*, *Sovereign of the Seas*, *Lightning*, *Red Jacket*, *Sea Witch*, *Young America*, *Challenge*, *Swordfish*—and, certainly, England's swift tea clippers, the *Thermopylae* and the *Cutty Sark*, to name but a few of the better known.

While this is more than a story of clipper ships or of sailing ships in general, it is not only appropriate but necessary to tell first of their great impact upon anyone or anything connected with the maritime business. The rise of our sailing ships coincided with the emergence and expansion of the country as a whole, and played a vital part in its swift and continuing growth. The first half of the nineteenth century provided opportunities for the making of vast fortunes, both on land and sea, through hard work and legitimate enterprise.

This could have then occurred only in the United States, with its large undeveloped territories and a free enterprise system. Moreover, the entire world was eager to share in our rapid advancement as a nation, and ports opened up to our trade on every continent. For this we required great numbers of ships, and trained captains and crews. If not overnight, this demand came about with sure and swift acceleration and with, seemingly, no limit to its potential. It was an opportunity that could come only once to any nation, one that many countries of the world had never experienced and could not in any future time.

Our response to it was immediate and extensive. We began to build ships by the hundreds, often developing the skills to do so with scarcely more than on the job training—yet they were ships that would get the job done. Farm boys became sailors, young men learned how to navigate and run a ship. There was an urgency to the whole business that seemed entirely out of character with our picture today of the more leisurely pace at that time. But it was a mighty task indeed, and to the everlasting credit of all concerned it was accomplished.

Without doubt, the color and vigor of America was best exemplified by the sailing ships of that period. Their voyages to lands never before seen by Americans opened our eyes and those of other nations as well, for nothing created by man had ever attained their grace and beauty. They challenged and generally overwhelmed England's best, bringing riches to our shores from exotic places that were virtually unknown to us until then. Sailing vessels of all sizes and rigging shipped out of ports from Maine to Baltimore, bound for foreign lands. The small towns of Salem, Marblehead, and Newburyport in Massachusetts vied with Boston and New York for the Far East trade, and whalers put out from New Bedford and Nantucket.

To indicate how truly young this nation is, just a few short years before the Revolution the province of Maine was still under periodic attack by the native Algonquin, a full hundred years after other Atlantic coastal areas had been settled and were growing in peace. Shipbuilding and sea trade, therefore, came into prominence much later in Maine. Once it had, the natural resources of the region and the growing skills and the energies of its people closed the gap rather quickly between it and its neighbors to the south—a triumph of wood and will, which we shall examine more closely in ensuing chapters.

Despite this delayed beginning and a preoccupation with the building of ships known as "downeasters," Maine was second only to Massachusetts in the number of clipper ships created in the fabulous 1850s. More than seventy were built in the state, with the little town of Damariscotta astonishingly accounting for nine of them. Massachusetts was far in the lead with nearly one hundred ninety, mainly built in Newburyport, Medford, and, of course, Boston, where Donald McKay completed twenty-one in a furious five-year period. New York, Baltimore, Portsmouth (New Hampshire), and Mystic (Connecticut) also ran. Philadelphia, an early leader in shipbuilding, never entered the race during the clipper ship years.

Donald McKay in East Boston and William Webb of New York were the acknowledged master shipbuilders of their time, and it is primarily to them that the credit must go for the building of the true clipper. It was the absolute in sailing ships, a masterpiece of wood and canvas, hemp and iron, and above all a living spirit. Here at last was a ship worthy not only of serving man, but of being served by him as well, proud enough, in fact, to demand the very best from him. It was amazing only that it had taken so many long centuries of shipbuilding to develop such apparent perfection—and then, finally, that it took place in young and still emerging America.

Yet the clipper ship did not appear suddenly, all of a piece. It was an evolution of sorts, over a period of at least ten years. The usually schooner rigged Baltimore clippers of the 1830s inspired considerable experimentation by designers and builders for square-rigged ships in the 1840s. Capt. Nat Palmer and John Griffiths, notable marine architects working independently in New York yards, were largely responsible for the development of the extreme, or true, clipper—a vessel with a sharp, narrow hull and trim lines, long tapering bow, and a particularly large spread of canvas on extended spars which, under full sail, made the ship appear almost top heavy.

Palmer, one of the best and most widely experienced shipmasters, used his sea knowledge and skills to full advantage ashore, and while no one man or particular group of men could lay claim to being the father of this lovely and precocious child, he and Griffiths played major roles.

Scarcely less important were the contributions of young Samuel Pook of New York. A consulting designer, Pook's first ship established his reputation in the field. She was the *Surprise* (1850); but it was the *Red Jacket* for which he is best known. This proud clipper joined McKay's otherwise exclusive "400 Club" on January 19, 1854, earning a place for herself and for her designer in the bright history of American sail.

From the *Rainbow* in 1845, and from several other early departures from the all-purpose packet ship type, came what many consider to have been the first recognizable clipper ship. She was the *Sea Witch*, designed by Griffiths and completed in 1846, Although her career at sea was a scant ten years, it was to be perhaps the most remarkable decade of sail in the history of the world.

She and the *Flying Cloud* (1851), considering their size, were the generally acknowledged all time champions, although larger ships with greater sail spread would later match or exceed some of their records. In 1853, for example, the year-old *Sovereign of the Seas* made a most memorable run under Capt. Lauchlan McKay, who was as adept a shipmaster as he was a builder. Donald McKay's new beauty became the first sailing ship to attain and exceed four hundred sea miles in a single twenty-four hour day. The significance of this is better understood upon learning that this was accomplished only twelve more times—and only once by other than McKay built ships, (Pook's *Red Jacket*). One such run was made by the *Great Republic*.

It is interesting that the *Great Republic* is included in such select company. Completed by McKay in 1853, she was by all odds the largest clipper ever built, measuring 4,555 tons, Her acres of sail towered to an average height of 200 feet above deck. She was an Amazon in the context of her time, and the entire shipping industry eagerly awaited her sailing. She was not fated, however, to fully realize her great potential. While taking on cargo at a New York dock for her maiden voyage she caught fire and burned to the water's edge.

The distraught McKay recovered in insurance only about half her cost of $300,000. Later she was sold and rebuilt, cut down in size and sail, and had a few excellent years at sea. What she might have accomplished in her original buxom form we can only imagine, but it would surely have been a most impressive career. That the *Great Republic*, the tallest ever of the tall ships, had been created by McKay was appropriate enough. Donald McKay was, and is still today, regarded as having been synonymous with the American clipper ship.

If it was an intriguing time to be alive in the rapidly growing America of the mid-nineteenth century, it was particularly so for a young man in coastal New England or New York. What a feeling of emotion must have filled such a lad seeing for the first time the full white sails and the sleek and graceful lines of a clipper ship gliding before him while entering or leaving port. Not a woman alive could have matched her haunting beauty or her promise of adventure—nor, indeed, the fatalistic fascination of her very existence for all men knew that on one voyage or another she could go down at sea or end up on some coastal reef with all hands lost.

That possibility, of course, rarely dissuaded the youth of her day. This was the peak period of American sailing ships, the spectre of steam-powered vessels not having yet seriously clouded the scene. Nor could anyone then envision the rapidly approaching catastrophe of the Civil War, which was to be the major factor in accelerating the advancement of the steam engine and the steel hull. Time was moving on in its deliberate way, but for the day of sail it was slowly and surely running out.

That darker side of the coin had existed all along with deadly certainty, as though its brighter face had blinded everyone to reality. Much sooner than most people had expected the toss was made, and the clipper and her sister sailing ships had lost. It took some years before the full impact of change manifested itself completely, and sailing ships struggled bravely on until they were, one by one, face to face with the inevitable. At last, like aging courtesans seeking only to survive, they were forced to submit to such humiliation and indignity as would have been unthinkable during their time of glory, their sails stripped down, their holds laden with coal or their decks with lumber, dragging along coastal lanes on slow and poorly paying hauls from one port to another.

Remembering her better days, it is easy now to forget that the race horse had been hitched to a junk wagon, that her sea routes to the Orient and to other foreign lands had been taken over by steel hulled steamers and that we had become almost entirely devoted to functional ugliness—or, that the great white birds had been shot down and consigned to the sentimental attics of our minds. While knowing why this had to be so, it was nonetheless sad and depressing—as it is, indeed, with the death of any great idea or ideal.

It is often supposed that the clipper ship faded out solely because of her limited cargo capacity. This was a definite factor, but the principal cause of her increasing disfavor was strictly a matter of cost. Her large spreads of canvas were expensive to maintain and replace, and required more crewmen to operate. Increasing her payload capacity to cover added cost would have sacrificed her sleek lines and the resulting swiftness for which she was designed.

The only answer, which quickly became evident, was an attempt to compromise between speed and capacity. (Maine would claim that she had known it all along, pointing to her success with the downeaster type.) At any rate, the clipper, as such, had reached her final port.

She lingered longer in Great Britain due to the tea trade with China, which had been for so many years the almost exclusive privilege of the smaller East India merchantmen, The famous *Cutty Sark* and other tea clippers were built after America's, but they too ended their days cut down in sail and plodding the seas to Australia and other lands with grain or whatever cheap cargo they could obtain.

The entire career of the clipper ship, as a definite type, had been all too short. In this country they were built mainly during the 1850s and were the queens of the sea for less than twenty years. For the remainder of the century square-riggers of the downeaster mold and large schooners continued to compete with steam driven ships. The beauty of sail, in evidence for so many centuries, reached its zenith with the clipper and died a slow and agonizing death thereafter.

In the later years of sailing ships the schooners, in fact, became more common than the square-riggers. They were considerably bigger than their earlier sisters, many having from four to six masts. The ultimate was attained by the steel-hulled *Thomas W. Lawson*, launched at Fall River, Massachusetts, in 1902. This imposing vessel was the only seven-masted schooner ever built, and she was truly a sight to behold on the open sea. Unfortunately, she was also clumsy and awkward, and difficult to handle in close quarters. Worse, because of her vast hold capacity it was next to impossible to get her a full cargo to anywhere. (By this time most of the bulk freight going by sea went via steamship.) In desperation she was converted into an oil tanker. The solution came with great finality when she went onto the rocks along the Scilly Islands, twenty-five miles off Land's End, in 1908. Her entire crew of fifteen went down with her.

The changeover from sail to steam, being a gradual process, produced some rather strange looking craft in attempts to compromise both methods of propulsion. There was an ultimate here, too. The *Great Eastern*, a paddle wheel and screw driven steamer of British construction, also carried six masts along her 693-foot length. Displacing 22,500 tons and with a 120 foot beam, she was many times larger than any other vessel of the period. Her sails, however, were almost never used, unlike many other combination ships upon which sail remained the principal means of propulsion as long as the winds blew.

The *Great Eastern* was distinctly one of a kind, and was used most notably during her career in the laying of the Atlantic cable in the 1870s. During her thirty active years she was primarily a passenger carrier, although never a financial success due to her high cost of operation.

What pass today for sailing vessels exist mainly for pleasure, at least in this country, and they can scarcely be compared to the ocean going sailing ships without which this continent could not have been settled by the white man for perhaps another two or three hundred years. What we, as a people and as a nation, owe to the daring seafarers of old is incalculable. The American Indian, of course, could have struggled along quite well enough without them.

Across inner Boston harbor from the East Boston waterfront, where McKay's clippers were built, stands a fifty-two foot monument to the famous shipbuilder. Near the shore on land-bound Castle Island, it overlooks the ship channel where many boats and ships must pass close by on entering or leaving the harbor. On one side of the granite marker a bronze plaque names every vessel built by McKay at East Boston—an impressive list indeed.

McKay's first clipper was the *Stag Hound*, launched early in 1851, followed closely by the *Flying Cloud*, still regarded as the best loved and most widely famous of all sailing ships. *Sovereign of the Seas*, a larger version of the latter, was a definite success, as were the *Donald McKay*, *Lightning*, and *James Baines*. The last named holds an all time record, a total of four times surpassing four hundred miles in a single day. *Lightning* has the record for one day: 436 miles.

Although the names of most of McKay's ships mean little to us today, the roster stands as a lasting tribute to the man who, in a few short years, gave us the most beautiful sailing ships ever created. There were, in that time, more than four hundred fine clippers built elsewhere along the Atlantic coast as well, whose names are rarely recognized now either, for most part, and no two of them exactly alike. But they were all a very special breed, and the least of them a work of art capable of firing the imagination and spirit as no inanimate masterpiece of painting or sculpture could ever hope to do. The irony here, we suppose, is that not one of them survives today in this country, whereas we still preserve and protect every ancient canvas or bit of marble by the great sculptors and painters of old, and rightly so.

Today, more than a hundred years after the fact, the great clippers still sail before our eyes in homes, offices, clubs—wherever pictures or models of them are displayed. Lacking wind or wave, each image is one that can be brought instantly to life in our imaginations, and once again the white sheets billow and strain, the bow dips and rises, and spray whips across the glistening deck lashing our faces with a salt wetness more exhilarating than wine. For some reason this full dimensional picture always seems to be that of the *Flying Cloud*, for although far from being the largest of the clippers she had such a vast spread of canvas that she appeared to be exactly that for which she was named.

No one has ever come close to adequately describing the great ships of sail, nor can we now. Artists have tried—endlessly, it seems—with limited success, for without motion their pictures cannot reveal the very essence of their being. Yet they certainly did exist, and in spite of the wonders of this most progressive of centuries, for us and as surely for generations yet unborn, there can never again be anything created by man as beautiful or exciting as the Yankee clipper, her smooth lines racing across the foaming blue with great white wings to the wind, heading out to the open sea for God knows where.

The clipper *Flying Cloud*

The clipper *Red Jacket* in the ice off Cape Horn in 1854

II
THE IRON MEN

To the Indies

*A hundred years
Of white sailed clippers,
A hundred years
To the Indies and back –
In your dreams, Captain,
In your long sleep.*

*How many ships
Do you sail, Captain,
How many ships
To the Indies and back,
In the haze and the mist
Of your long sleep?*

The loss of the sailing ships and of the craftsmanship that had created them was accompanied by another loss that has proven to be at least as far reaching in effect, for with their passing we also began to lose our concept of just how godlike a mere man could become. Upon his tiny ocean going world, a sea captain could attain a degree of respect approaching the super human—although, of course, none were supermen as we understand the word. This attitude toward complete authority was not uncommon at the time among men of position ashore, either, and while it produced many men of rare quality and worth, it likewise gave limitless power to others who proved incapable or corrupt.

Today our concern is much more toward humanizing men rather than deifying them. While this ongoing tendency is surely commendable, it, too, can be over extended, resulting in the opposite extreme, a loss of masculine powers and identity. The latter condition is one that could never have applied to any sailing shipmaster worthy of his command.

We do not suggest that all sailing ship captains were equally brave, wise, or skillful. Obviously this could not have been the case. All clipper and packet ship commanders, because of the great drive for speed, at times self imposed, did not in every instance measure up to their job, lacking the courage or swiftness of judgment in crucial moments, or in the necessary physical stamina. Those who failed, if they survived their ordeal, were quickly replaced. They may well have possessed all the skills and character desired, and may have been successful anywhere in any other field of endeavor, yet were destined to falter in this most demanding of positions.

It is no reflection upon present day sea captains to say, however, that the poorest clipper or packet shipmaster was probably better qualified than any captain is required to be today.

The very nature of a sailing captain's responsibility meant that a lack of outstanding courage and ability would have been fatal to himself and to his ship. There is no denying that sailing vessels were extremely vulnerable to the perils of the sea. The record is replete with tales of storm and shipwreck, of lost ships and men, and a captain who survived long years at sea required far more than good luck and favoring winds. He had to be thoroughly versed in seamanship, and have full knowledge of his ship, weather, and the handling of men. His world was a bobbing cork upon a vast ocean, prey to storms and fogs, winds and reefs, and it was his business alone to guide his craft safely from port to port, make his trades and return home with all hands, preferably with a handsome profit for his owners and himself. (From China, for example, tea, silks, and porcelain were obtained in exchange for whatever was acceptable in trade, usually silver, furs, sandalwood, or ginseng).

The Yankee trader captains knew what they wanted, and while it may have appeared that they sometimes received far greater value than they had given, the foreign merchants were hardly fools. The value of anything is great or less only to the degree that it is useful or desirable, and we can certainly assume that such was the view of the natives as well wherever we dealt with them. If there was a favorable balance for either of the bargaining parties it was an individual gain or loss, and that such was the case at times would have appeared to be inevitable.

We do know, at least, that our sea captains were rarely disappointed.

So the sailing shipmaster was often a businessman as well as a commander, expert seaman, and, while on duty, a virtual king of the limited world he trod upon. Some of this remains true of today's sea captain, although to a far lesser degree. Now he tends to be a much older man, as physical requirements today are obviously less than those needed in the days of sail, and seniority of service has become a major factor in attaining captaincy. And as a ship's crew is no longer at the complete mercy of its captain and officers it follows that the captain's role of authority has been considerably lessened.

A sailing captain often received his master's papers by the time he attained twenty-one, and more than likely had retired ashore at an age when a captain today is scarcely beginning his career as a master. Nor is as much left to the ingenuity and resourcefulness of the contemporary captain. While his technical skills are considerable, his individual responsibilities are far less. Navigation and seamanship remain basically the same as it has been for a hundred years, but the tools of a captain's trade are now vastly superior. (Can one imagine, for example, being in mid-ocean without so much as a radio contact?)

While the clipper was surely the queen of her saltwater empire, the packet ship was for many years the busiest of all sailing vessels along the Atlantic coast, plying regular routes on schedule with freight and mail as well as passengers, whether coastwise or trans-Atlantic. The Black Ball Line of New York was the first commercial packet line, with regularly scheduled sailings to and from Liverpool starting in 1818, followed by the Red Star Line in 1822 and by others in fairly rapid order on routes between coastal cities or to European ports.

Built for speed as well as capacity, the workhorse packet ship was driven, literally, by her captain to keep as near as possible to schedule or to exceed that time. It was an extremely hard and demanding life for the captain and crew alike, particularly during the winter months in the north Atlantic on the westerly run, where prevailing west winds of frequent gale force not only slowed progress but made any headway at all dependent upon the skill and resourcefulness of the captain. Yet the records of both ships and masters were remarkably good, and sailing time was shortened as the ships were improved in design and built larger. In absolute command while at sea, the captain rarely slept as he remained on duty throughout the voyage, at times literally strapped to his position on the bridge.

Fortunately, he was very well compensated for his efforts, and usually left this service after a few years to retire or to take up a much less demanding and hazardous enterprise.

Because of their particular skills and the overwhelming responsibility of their work, packet captains were regarded, with some awe, as a sort of professional elite. They were usually men of some financial means, often owners of businesses ashore, or were investors. On duty at sea they were under constant scrutiny throughout their voyages by passengers and crew alike, as they represented not only the line for which they sailed but their country as well. At that time the United States was competing heavily with England for commercial control of the Atlantic sea lanes, and every captain had a big stake in doing his best to see that his country kept foreign competition from taking over the lucrative Atlantic business.

* * * *

Maine had little to do with packet ships at the time, but she had far more than her share of sea captains. Many of them had been raised by rather strictly religious parents, and so were well acquainted with the Bibles they carried aboard ship. As were most lads of the period, they were brought up on hard work and responsibility. It was as though they had been poured into a mold from which there could be little deviation. If ever a man was bred to his time and occupation it was the Maine sailing ship captain.

Today we are inclined to believe that men are no longer as tough or as capable as the "iron men" of the clipper ship era. If this is true, it is largely because few men now have the sort of background and upbringing that their ancestors knew, either in this country or in many others overseas. Yet even were such a background to be provided, opportunities for individual responsibility in today's society are limited. While there are still persons of strong personal character among some business executives, political and military leaders, and the like, many others are largely dependent upon the contributions of those in supporting roles, sometimes to the point of being little more than figureheads, such as often graced the bows of sailing ships.

At any rate, it remains for us to look backward if we wish to see clearly what a man can become on his own merits. Although a high degree of what is now referred to as "old fashioned virtues"—sometimes in derision—were attributed to the sailing shipmasters, we actually know as little, comparatively, about their varied personalities as we do about the specific details of their careers. They were not, in the main, given to recording anything other than a few lines in their ship's log. Knowing the kind of men they had to be and the period during which they lived, however, we can conclude much about them for ourselves.

They were generally as stern and demanding as their position required them to be, with a strong sense of duty and a largely justifiable pride in their ability and calling. The captain often appeared as a rather vain and aloof figure on duty, dignified and sometimes dour and humorless, with absolute authority to make swift and unquestioned decisions. His officers and crew were required to work with him as a unit as their very lives depended upon the speed and skill of their cooperative action. This was not too difficult to manage during the years when a crew often consisted of home grown sailors who were frequently related to the captain and to each other. On packet ships and in the later years of nearly all sailing ships, when crews were mostly made up of whomever could be found at any port of call, including various and often incompatible nationalities, and types of men, the lot of the captain became much more difficult and severe measures of discipline were often necessary.

As far as can be assessed, there were few if any shipmasters from small towns along the Maine coast we could have considered in any sense tyrannical. On the whole they probably tended to be more personable and less demanding than the usual captain of the time, father figures to the young men who were often, as indicated, of their own or some related family. Yet the line between captain and crew was always maintained as a necessary part of the ship's operation, in fair weather or foul, and the success of a captain was in part measured by just how well he played his clearly defined role.

Among the sailing shipmasters, particularly in the earlier years, were many who made few voyages before retiring to the farm or to some other relatively safe occupation ashore.

Any list of captains includes those whose seafaring careers consisted of little more than single command, although in most instances they continued to revel in their title of captain for the remainder of their lives. Yet many others made the sea their home for twenty or thirty years or more, sailing all over the world in all seasons and wearing out several ships in the process. There were fortunes to be made, especially if one shared in the ownership of the vessel one commanded, as was often the case. Adventure and gold have lured men to undertake great risks throughout history, and a seafaring career offered ample prospects for both.

Many shipmasters retired after long or particularly astute careers at sea to fine homes filled with treasures obtained in the Orient and elsewhere abroad. Some of their descendants still live in affluence today as a result of the fortunes founded by their seagoing ancestors a century or more ago.

In the mid-1800s, the discovery of gold in California proved profitable to the east coast clipper ship owners and captains, for the three thousand mile trek across the still largely unsettled and Indian filled territories did not in any way appeal to those who mainly sought quick riches and the easy life. Many of those going west by ship chose to land in Panama and cross overland to the Pacific side where they continued by ship to California. Although the Panama isthmus was narrow in some places—as where the canal exists today—it was wild and barely passable at that time. More than a few travelers never made their connection on the Pacific side.

Along with passengers, ships bound for San Francisco "around the Horn" carried much freight. But the all sea route was not without danger to both ships and men. More often than not it was a very rough passage. This route was taken as well to South American ports and on voyages to the Far East, a long and trying course. Just as difficult, however, was the alternate route, not taken by those who were California bound, of course, but by ships going to China or the East Indies. This involved crossing the Atlantic and rounding the Cape of Good Hope before sailing eastward across the Indian Ocean.

There was simply no easy way to anywhere that required crossing large expanses of ocean.

Iron men indeed, and a good deal more, the captains of old. Many of them succeeded, however, in spite of having had little more than the barest formal education before going to sea at an early age. This is amply evident upon reading old sailing ship logs and letters written by shipmasters. While some were quite literate, few were any better educated than most working class lads at that time. Of much greater importance, their knowledge of the business in which they were so deeply involved was unquestionably complete or they could not have succeeded as so many of them did.

There is a tendency in a work such as this, involving the epic figure of great ships and staunch commanders, to give short shrift to the men who comprised the working crews of such ships. The ordinary seaman, whether native or foreign, had one of the most difficult and perilous of occupations, and little or no prospect of compensatory reward. The conditions under which he labored so long and hard were often nothing less than frightful, as demanding of an experienced old salt as for a stronger and younger man. Small wonder, then, that in the later days of sailing ships crews were made up of the very dregs of humanity, men with as little to lose as to gain and careless of either life or death—their own or anyone else's.

For many a long year the darker side of life at sea was accepted and largely overcome by men dreaming of ultimate command, or perhaps of nothing more than some free time in an exotic foreign port. Nor was the sea itself, in her lighter moments, an incompatible companion. If one had properly learned his duties and was physically fit to accomplish them, work could be satisfying and at times even pleasurable.

Normal shipboard life was not all work, of course. After a hard trick on deck there was usually time for some relaxation, and members of the crew often provided entertainment for themselves. Any musical instrument was welcomed, if no more than a sailor's hornpipe. Many an old salt had a colorful assortment of tales to tell, true or fancied, some of which were designed especially for the younger and more gullible sailors. Humor was necessary, as it has always been for men thrown together in war or in any situation of danger, hardship, or plain boredom.

Let the captain remain dour and aloof—he had his own problems, and it was neither customary nor necessary that he or the crew intrude upon each other's free time. During periods when a ship was becalmed—often for days—the morale of the sailors was heightened considerably if they were fortunate enough to have a good storyteller, singer or musician among them.

Any amusement to be had was their own doing, of course. Nothing was provided for the crew in the way of entertainment or recreation, nor was there much time for either on most voyages. The men expected and got little beyond their meals, space in which to sleep, and their pay. Most of them felt fortunate if they got those bare necessities. For all their hard work and the perils inherent in any trip to sea this was little enough indeed in the best of times.

Yet before the conditions of both the ships and the business itself had deteriorated, life aboard ship offered a challenge that men found stimulating to a far greater degree than any occupation they could have ventured upon ashore. Had this remained true, perhaps sailing ships would have lingered longer, in spite of the ever-present dangers on the high seas. One could not, in any case, fault the ordinary seaman for creating the conditions that led to the decline and fall of his means of livelihood. It was quite enough to risk one's life in a generally unrewarding job without having to be treated as a virtual slave as well.

We may be quite certain that if a crew was driven to the point of utter exhaustion at times, or suffered in any way, the captain shared their hard fate also. This, of course, in addition to his having full responsibility for the safety of both crew and ship. No captain worthy of his station asked more of his officers and crew than he himself was willing and able to give, and this deep pride in his strength and ability sometimes resulted in his own death at sea.

All aboard ship, from captain to cabin boy, had his own particular duties to perform, and the work and the risk was equally shared and understood by all concerned. Sailing ships were tiny little worlds in a vast space of ocean, completely out of touch with life beyond their own severe confines and it was a miracle only that so many of them made it from port to port as often and as long as they did. A large part of that miracle was human, of course—the magnificent men in the grand era of sail.

The square jawed captains of square-rigged ships remain bright in our imaginations today, not because they were larger than life but perhaps because we may now seem in many ways smaller than they. Part of this feeling may be due to the fact that their numbers were relatively few, while the individual of today seems rather lost in an ever-expanding society, whatever his position.

If it appears easier to stand out in a select group, however, it also puts a sharper focus and responsibility upon the individual, and this was surely true of the deep-water sea captain. By and large, he rarely failed to measure up to such attention. The best of the sea captains were a rare human equivalent of fire and ice, the sort of men the world has long sought among its leaders, and so seldom been fortunate enough to find.

III
TWO TOWNS IN MAINE

The Salt Coast

What is the sea
Without the land,
Or the land
Without the sea?
Here they end
Their loneliness
And become
As lovers;
Here an end
And a beginning,
And a timeless
Act of love,
Breathing life
From salt.

Long before the clipper ship made her first appearance, New England ports were busy in trade with the West Indies, South America, Europe, and the Far East. And by 1800, the craggy coast of Maine was becoming an increasingly active and important part of this growing maritime business.

  The short highly indented shoreline from Portland to Bath was bristling with the oaken ribs of ships in various stages of construction. Maine lumber was plentiful, and the coastline and larger rivers along most of the state were naturally suited to the building of wooden vessels of all types and sizes. Skilled workmen appeared seemingly overnight, and their numbers grew as quickly as did the need for them. The history of a small town can be rather heavy going, and we shall not dwell at great length here in telling the tale of Brunswick and Harpswell.

We are mostly concerned with the hundred years during which these two towns produced ships and seamen with an almost religious fervor, the only period of their history that would distinguish them from many other towns along the Maine coast—and even this is simply a matter of degree.

Brunswick, on the northern shores of Casco Bay, was incorporated as a town in 1738, after having had a couple of earlier settlements wiped out by Indian attacks. The town progressed steadily thereafter, and in 1802 its Bowdoin College held their first classes for a total enrollment of eight students. By that time Brunswick was becoming known as a shipbuilding town, and would continue as such well into the nineteenth century.

This was primarily accomplished by several generations of the Pennell family, culminating in forty years (1834-1874) of continued success at their shipyard in the section of town that has ever since been known as Pennellville. Seven of the family in one generation were builders at the yard, and it appears that James Pennell was the master craftsman of the lot.

Other members of the family were master carpenters for other yards as well, and some became well known shipmasters on their own vessels. James Pennell became a casualty of his trade, falling into the hold of a vessel under construction and suffering fatal injuries. Accidents of this sort were not uncommon in shipyards, on docks, or aboard ship, as the records show.

The Dunning family also contributed builders and captains quite early on—Robert and Andrew among the first shipbuilders, Samuel Dunning a generation or two later. The Given family, also early Brunswick settlers, was equally involved in both the building and sailing of ships. Most of the shipbuilding in Brunswick occurred at Middle Bay, Simpson's Point, and at Mere Point.

After the closing of the shipyards before the turn of the century, Brunswick became a mill town, and later the college town and shopping center for smaller surrounding areas that it is today. But it was built by early lumbering and shipping interests and it has never forgotten its heritage.

Perhaps it is appropriate that it is also the site of a major U.S. Naval Air Station[1], retaining at least a semblance of its nautical background.

Aside from this the only remaining links with her salty past are the grand old houses at Pennellville, tributes to the prolific family that had built them along with so many ships that these houses have managed to survive by many scores of years.

Harpswell, bordering Brunswick and jutting into Casco Bay, actually consists of one narrow peninsula and a number of islands. Three of the larger islands are strung together by short bridges, forming in effect a second peninsula alongside the one known as Harpswell Neck. The three adjoined islands are Great Island (East Harpswell), Orr's Island, and Bailey Island. Also included in the township are Birch Island and several assorted rocks, with few inhabitants beyond the summer months. As the year round population has never exceeded a scant two thousand residents it is particularly difficult to imagine today the furious activity in shipbuilding and seafaring that this little town proved capable of during the hundred years of Maine's greatest maritime production. Not incorporated until 1758, Harpswell soon caught up to her neighboring town of Brunswick in all phases of the building and the manning of ships.

There were a dozen shipyards in Harpswell, but the largest and most noted was that of George Skolfield, or Master George, as he was most aptly called. While his yards extended into Brunswick, Skolfield lived in North Harpswell and was considered a product of that town. In later pages we shall tell more of his works as they relate to members of his family and to other associated Harpswell builders and shipmasters.

Many ships that were built in the Harpswell area are known by name and type, although their builders are not listed. Records were kept rather haphazardly, it seems. Except for Master George's well-documented work, we find few others who carefully preserved such records. Among the exceptions were the yards of Curtiss and Estes—fourteen vessels built between 1848 and 1864—and those of Alcot Merriman and Norton Stover. Merriman's yard put out nineteen ships (1846-1882), and Stover contributed twenty-six from 1846 to 1879. These are minimal figures, as there were probably a few vessels among those built by unknown yards that should also be applied to their credit.

Isaac Snow was an early builder on Great Island, starting before the Revolution. Obviously, the maintenance of a shipyard on an island—even one only a short distance from shore, such as Great Island—

---

[1] The station closed in 2010.

presented serious problems in that period.

Only a few small vessels were ever built on Harpswell's Birch Island, closer to Mere Point than to Harpswell Neck. Birch Island was ideally suited in many respects, but Ebenezer Durgin completed two small craft there and that was it.

Hugh and Delight (Bailey) Meryman, whose farm home was for many years a place of great hospitality on Birch Island, left the building and sailing of ships to sons who moved to the mainland. One of them, Capt. Nathaniel, born in historic 1776, was among the family's first shipmasters.

* * * *

From early on Harpswell citizens had exhibited an uncommon zeal in the making of boats and babies. While these were undeniably the most popular pursuits nearly everywhere on the Maine coast, Harpswell had set out to become number one on a per capita basis. Whether or not it ever attained that prolific position, the town certainly gave its best shot. Boats grew up to become ships in every cove large enough to accommodate them, and a high percentage of the native offspring reached productive adulthood.

For several generations Harpswell went about its virile business as though it had received a mandate from God. Perhaps, eventually, it did. Harpswell's longtime pastor, Rev. Elijah Kellogg, was a personable and vigorous man, an expert sailor, and a writer of many books. If the town had needed inspiration to further its God-given ambitions, we suspect that he had been exactly the man to provide it.

* * * *

While the Brunswick-Harpswell area has not gotten too much attention in general histories of the sailing ship era in Maine, its contributions were many and deserve due credit. When the state surpassed every other in shipbuilding tonnage in 1855, these two towns accomplished far more than their share toward this outstanding record. Sloops, barks, schooners, brigs and ships came off their ways, most of them to be manned by captains and crews native to these towns, and often by members of the shipyard owners' families—if not by the owners themselves.

At first engaged mainly in West Indies and coastal trade, local ships expanded in size and numbers to a point where they became active in any port in the world open to receive them.

Aside from a goodly number of small boatyards, at least eighteen locations large enough to be classified as shipyards in Brunswick and Harpswell built nearly five hundred sailing vessels, mostly from 1780 to 1900. Some were sold new to outside interests, but most of them sailed from their homeport; after years of service many were, however, sold foreign rather than undergo extensive repairs for return voyages. In the later years of the nineteenth century this became a common practice among ship owners all along the coast as the increasingly high cost of maintenance and repair, coupled with the decreasing value of available return cargoes, made such sales an often necessary alternative.

* * * *

Casco Bay, it has been said, has as many islands as there are days in a year—someone must have counted every rock that showed itself at low tide. It is a truly beautiful area, glittering in the sun with all the opulence of a scattering of diamonds. Before the white man thrust himself upon its islands and shores, it was a favorite spot for Indian gatherings for, in all probability, many centuries. They would have been, above all, deeply appreciative of the clear waters of the bay, the invigorating air, and the multi-shaded greens of pine, spruce, birches and other trees that covered most of the land at that time.

This was the scene that the white settlers came upon and also found attractive. During the sailing ship period it remained relatively unspoiled, and in comparison with most of the bay or harbor areas in this country today it still appears fresh and bright. Portland is the only well populated and industrialized complex on the bay, which is so open to the Atlantic that, in spite of the many islands, its waters are not appreciably polluted.

Casco Bay, which has seen the entrance and departure of countless sailing ships since the late seventeenth century, has been in all that time a rare and sparkling setting for the clean white sails that have etched themselves forever upon its deep blue green.

* * * *

While we are primarily concerned with shipbuilders and sea captains from this one small section of the Maine coast it would hardly present a fair picture here were we to ignore the great importance to the country as a whole of the farmers, lumbermen, carpenters, and other tradesmen who left their homes to move westward during the mid-nineteenth century.

Scarcely a single family in Brunswick-Harpswell failed to contribute several of its members during these years to the large gatherings who pulled up stakes to travel west, bound for California and its gold fields, or to virgin farm lands that extended for more than a thousand miles beyond the western limits of the populated eastern states. Those who sought a fortune in California were generally the younger men. Families were more concerned with rich farmland or a good location where a town might be started and schools and churches built. Some of these families kept their destiny on the west coast, but far more settled in central or mid-western regions where their descendants still live today. The same drive and spirit of adventure that gave Maine so many sea captains equally moved others to become pioneers in the settling and building of the West.

Nowhere was the work ethic of the nineteenth century more pronounced than among the people of coastal Maine. Far more than the demands of mere survival or an independent spirit fostered their sustained energies. They were builders at bottom line, and expansion and profit was the name of their game. Their Scots-Irish-English heritage would not have permitted them to be content with anything less than fulfillment of their greatest potential to the absolute limit of their opportunities.

Calvinism may have been a harsh doctrine by today's standards, but it was well suited to the hardy pioneer stock of early New England we may well doubt that they could have prospered, or even survived, without their tough and abiding faith in God, and by extension, in themselves. It gave a cutting edge to their way of life.

Those who remained in Brunswick and Harpswell did not lack for opportunities either, at least until later in the century. While many of the ablest among the work force had left for wider horizons by that time, the French-Canadians of Quebec and Nova Scotia descended upon the state to provide new life and vigor, and there was no appreciable letdown in either the quality or the quantity of work in the area.

On the contrary, the newer element was largely responsible for the success of the mills in Brunswick, providing the town with an effective—if not long lasting—replacement for its declining shipyard industry.

One of Maine's most noted literary figures was Robert Coffin—Rhodes scholar, Bowdoin professor, writer, and poet. Much of his work lauded the self-sufficiency of the farmer fisherman of his Harpswell boyhood, the rugged natural beauty of the area, and a way of life that had—seen through his eyes—seemed almost idyllic.

Coffin was at least as enthusiastic about good Maine cooking—clambakes and such, plenty of lobster, and corn. In the end, it appears, the latter indulgence may well have done him in.

* * * *

Today, Brunswick maintains many active business interests in addition to its role as a college town, and unlike many other towns in the state has lost neither its modest prosperity nor its level of population. Harpswell remains largely residential in character, including a number of cottages for summer occupants. And Bailey Island's Mackerel Cove is a popular center and annual rendezvous for sports fishermen in pursuit of the elusive tuna.

There is no way that we can picture this section of Maine today as we know it appeared a scant hundred years ago. Yet if anything as masterfully built and majestic as the clipper ship could have disappeared so quickly, certainly all traces of wooden shipbuilding would have vanished over a much longer period of time.

The real pity, as we see it, is that records of ships and masters were not better kept and preserved for future generations to peruse and enjoy. Worse still, the true tales of their adventures, with rare exceptions, have also been lost to time. Yet they did exist, and it is our purpose to recall at least a few examples of that most worthy existence. For the rest, we leave it to the imagination of the reader. However vivid that may be, it can hardly overestimate its subject.

The Seekers

*They keep coming back
To the soil and the sea,
Back for a day
Where life began,
Needing the peace
And the strength of it –
Presidents, poets,
Shooters of stars –
They all come back,
Knowing they must,
For a fistful
Of living earth,
Or the salt taste
Of windblown spray.
Always and always
The great seekers
Keep coming back.*

IV
BUILDING THE SHIP

From the days of the first settlements along the Maine coast, boats have been a necessity, both for fishing and for transportation. Early roads—what few there were—were no more than narrow country lanes that were often impassable in bad weather.

Islanders, of course, relied entirely upon their boats. The coastal, or "salt water" farmers went fishing and lobstering for a good part of their food supply. Dugout canoes, dories and skiffs were used, and sail made its appearance with the small sloops that were built as fishing grounds were extended. The farmer-fisherman, experienced in the use of hand tools—many of them having built their own houses and farm buildings—learned how to build their boats as well.

The necessary prelude existed prior to the inception of shipbuilding, as lumbering became important to the region's economy as soon as settlements were established. Masts and spars were produced in great quantity for the Royal Navy, and this led toward their production for local use.

While colonists at that time had no thought of becoming independent of England, their own progress was dependent upon themselves in this newly settled and still remote region. So it was a most natural progression, then, that from lumbering and from the building of their own fishing boats came the first small shipyards along the Maine coast.

Walter Meryman came to Harpswell in 1738, following a seven-year indenture learning the ship carpenter trade at Cape Elizabeth. From him, and from others who learned their skills early, came several generations of master craftsmen who provided Harpswell and its vicinity with shipwrights. And there were many house carpenters who, with only rudimental training, adapted their talents to become ship carpenters.

The shores of Brunswick and Harpswell were ideally suited for shipbuilding, with deep-water coves and a fine source of oak, pine, and other timber available. Fieldstone for use as ballast was plentiful. The natural setting was there, awaiting only the development of the skills needed to put shipyards into full operation.

Over these early years of trial and error came the nucleus for what was to become the major industry in the state for many years. (We use the word "state" in current reference, well aware that Maine did not attain full statehood until 1820.)

It was not until the Civil War period that Maine began to doubt the future of sailing ships. Old timers in the business held out their hopes considerably longer. But in the early years of the nineteenth century there was never any doubt whatever that ships would be built in Maine forever, that its coastline would be one continuous spread of shipyards with its citizens engaged in maritime activities in ever increasing numbers. There was no substantial reason to believe otherwise.

The future seemed limitless, and Maine gloried in her growing power and prestige. God had been more than kind, placing her hardy breed in this fortuitous land at such a propitious time in history. Maine envied no other part of the country, certainly not her neighboring states to the south in spite of their having had earlier advantages. The storied independence of Mainers was greatly bolstered in these optimistic years, and did not diminish as did her fortunes by the twentieth century. If they were a stubborn lot, was that not one of the reasons they had succeeded so well in the first place, both at home and wherever they wandered?

It had been, of course, far from an easy beginning. For many a long year lathes and other power tools were unknown in Maine, and the available hand tools often lacked finish and required working on to become suitable for use on fine and detailed work. Broad axes, adzes, whipsaws, cross-cut saws, chisels, hammers and sledges, lever bars, planers, caulking mallets—the ring and the whirl, the sounds of tools in the hands of ever more experienced shipwrights and the song had begun. All operations involved hand labor at first and so it remained well into the nineteenth century. Soon master ship carpenters were gaining a respect and importance in their communities as leading citizens that would stand up for generations to come.

After the War of 1812 and the lifting of the embargo on shipping, Maine began to make her move as a power on the seas. Whereas ports in Massachusetts and New York were having more than difficulty recovering, Maine was scarcely beginning, in shipbuilding and in the training of sea captains and able mariners.

The embargo had been thoroughly despised by everyone connected with sea trade along the Atlantic coast, and although they had less to lose than long established ports in other states, Maine shippers, builders and seafarers were as angered by Thomas Jefferson's embargo as any—necessary as that act may have been.

Nowhere, it should be remembered, was there a breed of men more aware of dollar value or more concerned with acquiring said dollar than the working businessmen along the Maine coast at that time. For that matter, the average shipyard worker and sailor had been at least as greatly affected, many of them forced to return to the farm or to house carpentry for their living.

It had been a relatively brief interruption, of course, and ships continued to increase in size and improve in design under progressive shipbuilders, culminating in the great clippers built by the Nova Scotian brothers, Donald and Capt. Lauchlan McKay, at East Boston. Maine turned to the downeaster type as well, a full rigged ship broader of beam than the clipper and a larger cargo carrier, sacrificing little in speed in many instances although carrying shorter sail.

The Pennells and Skolfields and other shipbuilders in Brunswick and Harpswell, being largely self-taught, developed their skills without frequent use of some of the more sophisticated methods that emerged in Boston and New York. They continued, for example, to use treenails (trunnels) instead of iron bolts in the outer planking and ceiling (inner planking), as well as in the joints that curved upward from the keel.

The actual building of a ship began with molds, or patterns, made of wood from designs worked out on paper to the last detail. The laying of the keel on blocks, on a nearly level area usually a very short distance from the water, was followed by the fitting of the curved joints from stem to sternpost. When the main pieces of the frame had been erected and adjusted in accordance with their molds, the inner and outer planking was applied.

The larger and more advanced yards followed the latest and most scientific methods, involving a detailed use of mathematics, geometry and trigonometry, and special shipwright slide rules. This is not to say that the local Maine yards ignored technical progress as such, merely that they favored, when applicable, their own system of rule of thumb, which, as their finished products amply verified, were effective in both design and durability.

Up to the point of launching, Brunswick-Harpswell ships were entirely the work of their builders. The fitting out with sail and rigging, however, was left to professionals in Portland or Bath, as the work of the local yards ended with the staying of the masts and the painting of the vessels.

A detailed account of the building of a ship would require a full volume of particulars, of interest only to someone intent upon building one for himself. The work, as accomplished in the early Maine shipyard days, was hard and often disagreeable. As construction was effected entirely out-of-doors, winter weather played a generally negative role in work schedules. Working hours were long and wages no better than that of any industry at that time. Master shipwrights, naturally, fared somewhat better than less skilled workers, being craftsmen and having more responsibility for the end results of their labors.

As ships were built larger they also required more work beyond the early stages of construction. Two, or even three, decks became relatively common, and ornate figureheads and other decorative material and designs were often added. (Characteristically, some Maine builders did not become too involved in this sort of thing.) Many of the improvements came about as a result of the clipper ships, for although they did not last long as a class they gave builders the benefit of their good points as well as their deficiencies in designing new models.

The downeasters, and later large schooners, became the most popular sailing vessels, but all too soon the die was cast and builders were turning more and more to the fishing and pleasure craft field. Wooden shipbuilding was approaching full cycle at last.

It is ridiculous to suppose that a few brief paragraphs can properly cover this grand period in Maine shipbuilding, even on the small section of the coast we are concentrating upon. A much longer and more expansive account is needed, in spite of the lack of names and dates that should be included. To span the entire Maine coast such a work would involve years of research, and while it might be helpful it could not be complete as a factual record. Rather than bemoan this fact let us take the information at hand and apply it in connection with other chapters to create a representative picture of this time and place. An abstract, as any artist would admit, is quite as likely to present a true picture as one involving minute detail and may, indeed, evoke greater feeling.

As many of us are not familiar with the different types of sailing craft and their rigging it might be appropriate at this point to define them. There were numerous variations, to be sure, but essentially they were as follows:

SHIP - three square-rigged masts.

CLIPPER - ship rigged, but with a larger sail spread and a sharper, narrower hull.

BARK - three or four masts, square-rigged except for a fore-and-aft rigged after mast.

BRIG - two square-rigged masts.

BRIGANTINE - square-rigged foremast, fore-and-aft rigged after mast.

SCHOONER - two or more fore-and-aft rigged masts.

SLOOP - one fore-and-aft rigged mast.

We cannot in good conscience conclude this chapter on shipbuilding without telling something of Brunswick-Harpswell's contemporary rivals, Yarmouth and Freeport. On the shores of Casco Bay between Brunswick and Portland, they were also busy shipbuilding towns for many years during the sailing ship era.

Portland and Bath operations would require a volume or two to properly report. Bath, of course, has continued to build ships since the earliest days of the town, notably during both World Wars, and is presently an important producer of nuclear submarines. [2]

Both Bath and Portland—earlier called Falmouth—had much to do with the fame of Maine sailing ships and their records are quite well documented in existing books on the subject.

Yarmouth, although active in shipbuilding as early as any other Casco Bay community, hit its stride with the establishment of the

---

[2] Since 1995, Bath Iron Works has been a subsidiary of General Dynamics, and the facility is now devoted to the construction of complex surface combatants for the U.S. Navy.

Blanchard yard in 1848 and with the Hutchins and Stubbs yard two years later. Capt. Sylvanus Blanchard, with his sons and associates, continued to build for thirty years. Hutchins and Stubbs remained active until 1884. Blanchard had the distinction of producing the largest ship ever built in the town. She was the 2,209-ton *Admiral*, the only sailing vessel at the time boasting iron masts and spars.

Freeport shipbuilding competed on at least even terms with Yarmouth, much of its early work accomplished by the Porter family. In 1847, Rufus Soule took over operations at Porter's Landing and for the next dozen years or so turned out a large number of craft. The biggest yards, however, were those of Briggs and Cushing, and the Soule Brothers at Strout's Point, run primarily by Capt. Enos Soule.

The latter yard was in business from 1839 until 1877, and their ship *Tam O'Shanter II* (1875) became the best known of all vessels built in either Yarmouth or Freeport. Her sea career lasted twenty-four years and included some spectacular races against ships of comparable size. The Briggs and Cushing yard produced Freeport's largest, the *John A. Briggs*, among the many they turned out in the years between 1855 and 1880. During most of this period George Anderson was the master carpenter at the yard. While all shipyards had capable shipwrights heading up their operations, Anderson's longevity and craftsmanship was second to none along the Maine coast.

The definite but friendly rivalry of shipbuilders and master carpenters and of one town with another was matched as well by shipyard workers at nearly all levels. For many of them it was a great distinction and source of pride to be considered one of the best joiners, riggers, caulkers, or carpenters in Maine. And to be so rated was no small feat, as there were large numbers employed in all trades connected with the building and outfitting of sailing ships throughout this era of consistently high production.

Having seen pictures and models of early shipyards we can appreciate the vast amount of hand labor that went into the creation of each vessel, of whatever size. The mere thought of it is enough to give one callouses and a perpetual backache. The pace of individual workers may not have been fast in comparison with assembly line workers today in many industries, but any rate of speed sustained from dawn to dusk, six days a week, was tough enough.

And if we are to believe the generally superior quality of the craftsmanship involved—as the records of ships that survived long years seem to prove beyond doubt—we have to say that the old boys did some kind of job. Call it pride, or whatever motivated them to accomplish the seeming impossible, ships did get built in incredible numbers year after year.

A master ship carpenter had as much right to be proud of his title as any sea captain had to be of his, and in some instances perhaps a good deal more. I am reminded of one visit I made to Harpswell's old cemetery. On one of the gravestones, the name of the man was preceded by "Captain"—and I knew full well that he could not have had but a very short time at sea. Nearby was a stone with the name of a man who had given a lifetime to the building of ships, a master at his trade—just a name and dates, and nothing more. I felt that it should also have been deeply inscribed, "Master Carpenter"—little enough to say for any man who had done so much to help shape Harpswell's great record in the days of sail.

All master shipwrights had a special pride in, and feeling for, every vessel their skilled hands completed. We may imagine the tremendous satisfaction they must have felt upon seeing their ships, rigged out and under full sail, ready for their maiden voyages. And we can as readily understand the terrible loss they must also have felt when one of their own creations was lost at sea on that first voyage, which happened on occasion.

But this, of course, is another story, as necessary to the complete picture here as natural disaster and death are to life itself. This analogy is more appropriate than most, for each sailing ship was looked upon as a living being, complete with an inner spirit akin to the human soul. And each vessel was as much an individual, each with distinctive characteristics, quite unlike any other. Sailors, notably superstitious, compared them to women, known or imagined, and invariably classified them—wild, gentle, capricious, sluggish, frisky—or just plain lucky or unlucky.

Once a ship had been so labeled the word quickly got around among the seamen and had some bearing upon their desire to ship aboard, or not to do so. (The reputation of the captain had at least an equal effect in attracting or repelling voluntary enrollment for sea duty.)

Maine had the timber in wood, and the right timber in men, and one complemented the other. There was a feeling in working with wood that none of the old shipbuilders could find working with metal. Few of them made such a changeover, preferring retirement to learning an entirely new way of building a ship. The choice was rather academic anyway, as few shipyards in Maine continued to operate once orders for wooden vessels stopped coming in.

Bath carried on, and later became once gain a leading east coast builder with its Bath Iron Works. But up and down the coast of Maine, as the century came to a close, there was little left of its once busy shipyards. Over the years they remained silently rotting away, fewer reminders of their glorious past left each spring following the long winter's snow and ice. The last of their sailing ships continued on until they, too, came to final rest along vacated docks, or were beached on shores many hundreds of miles from their places of launching.

Perhaps the ships that went down at sea during the happier days of sail were the lucky ones. And no doubt some of the old tars who shared their fate felt the same way. For the ships, it was never a choice. Their age was seldom a factor, nor was their size; storms could as easily capsize and sink the finest craft afloat as they could a battered old sloop, given the right conditions.

Nor were many of the captains who were lost at sea in any way neglectful of their duties or lacking in ability. The full power of the sea and of the winds, when aroused, was enough to destroy an entire fleet of sailing ships had they been in the wrong place at the wrong time. But the oceans being incredibly vast, it was a rare occasion when more than one or two ships were lost during a single storm.

As every ship was given life, so that life eventually ended, soon or late, gracefully or with brutal suddenness. Having spent some time with the building of them it is now time to tell how many of them came to swift and tragic ends.

Bark *I. L. Skolfield* – built in Skolfield Yard, Brunswick, 1879

Ship *Sam Skolfield II* – built in Skolfield Yard, Brunswick, 1883

V
THE FLIP SIDE

One of the more fascinating aspects of the sailing ship era for most people is the record of shipwrecks and other nautical disasters. Yet the loss of life alone, including many of the finest young men ever to put out to sea, was in no way one of the more glorious chapters in an otherwise progressive story. All too often the names of these brave lads were followed in family records by such terse notations as "drowned," "lost at sea," or "washed overboard." Some were more specific, as "lost off Cape Horn," or "died at Guadeloupe."

As far as the loss of ships was concerned, they were not built to last beyond a rather specified period of time at best, of course, however well constructed. The manner of their passing was distinctly a secondary consideration. With any sort of luck a ship would last long enough to make money for her owners. Many were sold time and again before ending up in a state of ruin and decay, quite often on some foreign shore.

While this sort of finish may not have been as dramatic as that of a ship gone down at sea, there were stories within their decaying hulls as well, tales that would for the most part never be told. (As a boy at Winthrop Beach, Mass., I recall playing above and below the decks of one such derelict schooner ending her days ingloriously alongside an equally neglected and rotting pier. I did not consider where she might have sailed, nor where she hailed from, but there was an eerie feeling that she was inhabited by the spirits of the sailors who had trod her decks when she was still a seaworthy vessel.)

The stories of ships going down at sea or smashing up along shore in fog or storm are endless. The number of vessels that left port never to be heard from again was also surprisingly large. (Ghost ships, too, have long been a favorite subject for writers and poets. They are certainly featured among the many tales told by my fellow Harpswell descendant and former townsman, Edward Rowe Snow, the prolific storyteller of New England's historic coast.)

Disaster was a way of life for the wives and families of the seafarers, and often struck several times in one family. Capt. Benjamin Henly, for example, lost two of his four shipmaster sons to the sea.

Capt. Benjamin Adams, a victim of his hazardous occupation, had a son to take his place before the mast. His granddaughter, however, and her husband, young Capt. Vincent Given, went down together on one fatal voyage.

But the list of the lost is eternal. The sea will claim its victims always, sail or not, as it has from earliest times. Yet the siren call of the white sailed ships was particularly alluring to men and boys alike. It was certainly not the money involved, as a merchant seaman at that time would expect no more than twenty or thirty dollars a month while at sea. And all were well aware of the dangers of shipwreck and, perhaps worst of all, fire at sea.

At this late date we can dismiss the monetary losses of ship owners rather easily, and disaster at sea takes on an interest for us that has always been a rather curious aspect of human nature. It is, nonetheless, a part of life and, unfortunately, a vital part. We do not wish to dwell upon the subject at great length, nor indicate any of the near accidents of which there were many.

On the other hand, we cannot emphasize too strongly the tragic nature of seafaring in the days of sail, which serves, it would seem, to illustrate the fascination the sea held for so many young men. They were, in the halcyon years, eager to go to sea, whether for one voyage or many. Nor was it unusual to read of one going down with his ship when eventual rescue may have been at least possible. Such an act by an ordinary seaman would seem to suggest the love such a man held for his ship, greater than some would have for a human counterpart. Examples of fatalistic courage during disaster, while never common, were far too numerous to put down as exaggeration or romanticism.

While the decline of the sailing ship may be rightly attributed to the development of steam power and steel hulls, it would seem amply evident that wooden ships were always a calculated risk for their owners, the shippers of cargo, and for all who sailed them. If we have taken some justifiable pride in the beauty and speed of sailing ships we must also admit their shortcomings. The very nature of sail precluded the establishment of any reasonably exact sailing time between ports;

the presence or lack of wind obviously governed such time, and long calms often resulted in delays of many days. And the all too frequent losses of the vessels themselves and of valuable cargo was certainly far too great in proportion to their numbers and to the tonnage transported.

What follows is a chronological list telling the fate of some Brunswick-Harpswell ships that may be of some interest due to the nature or the location of the incidents. These are but a few authentic disasters, natural or deliberate. While they are rather terse reports and lacking in detail they do present the essential facts. No great amount of imagination is required to fill in the gaps. (What does strike us is that so many ships were lost to Confederate war vessels during the Civil War. This was a phase of that war that we read little about as school children, remembering mostly the action in southern waters and the victories of Admiral Farragut. Doubtless southern textbooks were as much inclined to play up their own successes while minimizing their losses as well.)

Brig *Guadeloupe* - Left Portland on her maiden voyage; lost on Dec. 14, 1844, with all hands.

Bark *Natchez* - Abandoned at sea with a cargo of ice, out of Boston for New Orleans, Jan. 2, 1845. The crew was picked up and landed at LeHavre, France. (The cargo, we may well assume, eventually melted.)

Bark *Oregon* - On her first voyage, Jan. 30, 1846, wrecked on Nauset Beach, Cape Cod, with a full load of cotton.

Ship *Jacob Pennell* - From Mobile for Liverpool with cotton, came ashore at Wexford, Ireland, on Feb. 22, 1846, with her rudder carried away and with masts and rigging overboard to port. The ship was a total loss, her crew and cargo saved.

Brig *Mary Pennell* - Lost on Jan. 22, 1849, with a load of coal at Chagres, Panama.

Brig *Pinta* - Abandoned at sea, March 11, 1851, out of New York for Havana. The crew was rescued and landed at New York City.

Ship *Joseph Badger* - On June 4, 1851, out of New Orleans for Liverpool loaded with cotton, burned at anchor in the Southwest Pass of the Mississippi River—a total loss.

Ship *James Pennell* - She was abandoned Nov. 23, 1852, off Cape Horn, eastbound with a cargo of grain, which shifted in heavy seas. The vessel listed and the crew abandoned ship, were rescued and landed at Valparaiso. Apparently another heavy sea shifted the cargo and righted her as she was later seen sailing southward, seemingly undamaged and with no one aboard. Heavy weather prevented a salvage attempt, and she sailed away toward the open Atlantic never to be seen again.

Bark *Clement* - Went ashore in a southeast gale in April 1856, breaking up on Narragansett Beach while en route from Baltimore to Boston.

Bark *Tedesco* - From Cadiz, Spain, with a valuable cargo (sherry, etc.), bound for Boston. During the night of Jan. 18, 1857, a very sudden and violent northeast storm developed, taught on a lee shore, she was wrecked on a rock off Lynn Beach, with no survivors. In the morning wreckage, cargo, and the bodies of the crew were scattered along what is now named Tedesco Beach—less than twenty miles from her intended destination.

Schooner *Benevolence* - On Jan. 26, 1857, she anchored in the lee of Chebeague Island in Casco Bay, late in the afternoon, to ride out a heavy northwest gale. By daylight she had disappeared and no trace of either vessel or crew was ever seen again.

Ship *Africa* - Lost en route from Cardiff, Wales, for Shanghai on Aug. 31, 1860. The crew was rescued and landed at Singapore.

Ship *Cornelia* - Foundered twenty-five miles north of Sicily on April 14, 1861.

Clipper Schooner *Grandilla* - Abandoned at sea en route from New York to New Orleans with general cargo, March 21, 1860.

Ship *A.B. Thompson* - Captured off Savannah on May 18, 1861, and burned, by *C.S.S. Lady Davis*. Taken to Charleston and sold. On April 4, 1862, she was filled with sand and sunk in the channel entrance to Savannah Harbor, an effort to prevent entry by Union warships.

Bark *Greenland* - Captured and burned off Hatteras by the *C.S.S. Florida*, on July 9, 1864.

Bark *P.C. Alexander* - Burned by C.S.S. Tallahassee off Monhegan Island en route home from Cuba on Aug. 16, 1864.

Brig *Albion Lincoln* - Captured and burned by the *C.S.S. Chickamauga*, 300 miles southwest of New York on Oct. 13, 1864.

Ship *Sam Dunning* - After ten years of successful operation, and while en route from Rangoon to Liverpool, she ran into a severe typhoon in the Indian Ocean, with a full cargo. Although she had apparently weathered the seas in good order, the large quantity of rice in her holds began to swell from water seepage, and the hull was split open. In the ensuing sinking twenty-five of her officers and crew were lost, including the captain. The remaining six found refuge on the floating deckhouse. After several days of suffering from thirst in the hot sun, two men drank salt water, went out of their minds and jumped overboard. On the sixth day the remaining four men decided to draw lots to see who should be killed for his blood and flesh. At this most opportune moment a ship appeared on the horizon and came close enough to see and rescue them. The date of this quite remarkable ending, following the even more unusual accident to the ship itself, was April 9, 1865. The survivors were landed at Point deGalle, Ceylon.

Ship *Brunswick* - Captured and burned by the *C.S.S. Shenandoah* on June 28, 1865, in the north Pacific. Her crew was taken aboard by two nearby ships, some of them landing at Honolulu, the rest at San Francisco.

Bark *Addie Decker* - In January 1868, she was driven ashore and lost near Vera Cruz, Mexico.

Bark *Istria* - Lost on Diamond Shoals, off Cape Hatteras, with a cargo of cotton, hides, and staves. All but four of the crew were lost. Date was July 11, 1868.

Brig *Josephine* - From Portland for St. John, New Brunswick, Aug. 9, 1871, wrecked on Sand Island at the mouth of the Machias River with a cargo of flour.

Bark *Deborah Pennell* - On Dec. 20, 1873, from Baltimore for Rotterdam, ran ashore in a fog and became a total loss on the Banjaard, a reef off the Dutch coast. Yet another loss for the Pennels, who by this time must have been running out of family names for their ships.

Bark *Caroline Lemont* - Lost on the coast of Chile, en route from Buenos Aires to Valparaiso, on Dec. 22, 1873.

Bark *Anglo Saxon* - From England bound for San Francisco, wrecked on the coast of Uruguay in November 1877.

Brig *Anita Owen* - Lost Dec. 1, 1885. Heading for Boston Harbor, she was caught in a heavy northeast gale and was unable to make port. The captain elected to anchor outside the breakers off Nantasket Beach. That night the cable parted and she drove ashore. All hands were rescued by the surfboat; the brig was a total loss.

Schooner *Billow* - Lost on the Isles of Shoals on Jan. 6, 1896, bound from Owls Head, Maine, for Richmond with a cargo of lime.

Ship *Benjamin Sewell* - Lost on the Pescadores Reef off the Formosa coast, Oct. 6, 1903. The crew reached shore on Botel Tobago Island, only to be killed by the natives. (Built in 1874, the *Benjamin Sewell* was the last ship launched at Pennellville.

Perhaps it is just as well that we have come to the end of this list of unfortunates. How many ships can one sink in a few pages? Yet these were but a few Brunswick-Harpswell ships to leave their homeport never to return. No doubt there were many wild but true tales among those that remain unknown to us today.

Ghost ships—unmanned vessels that roamed the seas for varying lengths of time—certainly existed in fact and were not mere figments of writers' imaginations. Mutiny and piracy accounted for some of the missing ships; there was seemingly no end to the number of ways they could sail out of the picture and not be seen again.

Within the memory of our oldest citizens most of the Atlantic coast was a veritable graveyard of sunken or beached sailing ships, their waterlogged remains slowly breaking up.

Today virtually nothing is left to be seen of them anywhere, yet the ocean bottom holds far more than a scattering of shapeless timbers covered by various forms of marine life. It keeps forever the dreams of countless men—brave sea captains, promising young sailors, old salts looking only for a few years of storytelling retirement ashore. Neither their dreams nor their lives will ever be forgotten, for they gave all for their land as surely as the men who died in wars to gain or preserve our freedom.

They were the frontiersmen of the sea, exploring, reaching, seeking—casualties of our quest for trade and knowledge all over the world. Others attained what they did not survive to accomplish, but they deserve an equal standing among the heroes of American history. Lost ships and men were the prices we had to pay for our progress as a nation and for the respect of other countries with which we exchanged goods and ideas. Overall, we have to conclude that the cost, however great, was not too unreasonable.

VI
THE COASTAL CLANS

Father

Always the sea,
The golden wave
In the sun,
Silver crossing
The black at night,
The green, the blue,
The white.
Always the sea,
While men scream
And die across
The centuries;
Always the sea,
Giver of life
And indifferent
To laughter or tears.

From the earliest time of man the sea has been a fascinating mystery, a restless and moody mass of salt water with, seemingly, a life entirely its own. During these same long ages man contemplated its mysteries and sought the means by which he could unravel some of its secrets. Thus was born the sailor, the daring explorer, so far back in time that we have no idea today when he first put out to sea, or from where.

But sea exploration and travel has always been secondary to the more pressing need of sustenance. Doubtless the first boats ever built were created for fishing, and countless venerations in coastal and island areas the world over have spent their lives in pursuit of seafood. Yet regardless of the reasons they went to sea, certain families developed an affinity for life on salt water and would not have been content without it. The builders of boats and ships likewise passed their skills and feeling for their work on to sons and grandsons.

Not a man yet has been literally born with salt water in his veins, or the taste of it in his mouth. A deep love for the sea and for sea related occupations were most often developed over a period of time, usually beginning out of sheer necessity.

This is shown most clearly in our story of maritime life in early Maine. In a matter of but two or three generations settlers firmly established family traditions of shipbuilding and seafaring that would continue for a hundred years or more.

Fishing and lobstering have been important to Maine's economy since the earliest coastal settlements. For more than two hundred years lobstermen hauled their traps by hand, rowing from one buoy to another in the time honored manner and enjoying an independence that few men in any business have known since.

Today, motorboats equipped with winch and davit, haul a far greater number of pots, strung together by trawl lines, in a single day. And the lobsterman now has little voice in setting the price he can get for his catch in the market. Lobstering, too, has become big business, and conservationists are concerned.

But in the period of which we write, fish of many kinds were plentiful along the Maine coast. They provided a good part of the food supply for coastal and island dwellers, and some income as well. And their boats, as we have seen, were the forerunners of the sailing craft that were soon to be built in such great numbers in Maine. Thus the ancient role of the fisherman played an important part in the birth of a fast growing new industry.

Every coastal town or village had its seafaring families, generations whose fishing or sailing careers overlapped each other's for a century or two. They were the salty ones, as hard working and independent as were the cowboys of the Old West. Like the cowhands of the plains, they labored long and anonymously, savoring the rough-hewn ways of outdoor living in all seasons and proud of their fellowship with nature and the clean free atmosphere of their work. There was a sense of continuity, of a oneness with all life past and contemporary, and a confidence in themselves that could have come only with the certain knowledge that they were making their own way and were beholden to no one. This characteristic was common to New Englanders at the time, and still persists today among some inhabitants not necessarily descendants of early native stock.

There is no way, really, to separate boat and shipbuilding, fishing, commercial seafaring, or even a naval career. All water related activities involved entire families in one or several such categories for generations along the Maine coast and beyond.

The Alexander family, one of the earliest in Brunswick-Harpswell, was well represented in recent years by William T. Alexander (R. Adm., U.S.N.R.), continuing his family's seafaring tradition. His history of Harpswell, featuring the town's shipbuilding past, provided a reliable source of information that contributed to several chapters herein.

Harpswell's preoccupation with the building and the sailing of ships was hardly surprising as the township is almost entirely surrounded by salt water. Its early inhabitants, though, almost without exception, had no previous experience or family background in things nautical. Most of the settlers of the region were Scots-Irish from Ireland, Puritans from Massachusetts, and colonists from other Maine settlements. Wherever they came from, they were quickly thrust into the rugged life of the Maine coast, which meant, for many of them, involvement with ships and/or the sea.

In later years, as these activities diminished and interests of the younger generations turned westward, their early habits of hard work and responsibility under often difficult conditions gave them the necessary fortitude and experience to begin and sustain their lives in new lands. Thus, in a very real sense, their salt water heritage became a part of this country from Maine to California. It is very likely that, today, there are more people of Maine coastal descent living in California than are left of the early families in Maine.

This toughening process was by no means the exclusive upbringing of northern New Englanders, nor were they in the majority of the pioneers who settled the West. Of course, they never claimed to be; State of Mainers would be the last to take undue credit for anything, whether they were at home or in any other place.

Brunswick-Harpswell shipbuilders and sea captains included members of nearly every family in those towns. Many families were so closely related, in fact, that they appeared to be one single clan, which became a definite factor in their progress. Yet a strong feeling for the sea was noted in some families far more than in others.

The Pennells and Skolfields produced builders and captains with equal facility. The large Pennell family built no less than eighty vessels of all types, probably a great many more for which records are missing or fragmentary. The most notable individual success was undoubtedly that of George Skolfield (1780-1866). His yard was in operation from about 1820 until 1885, and was run by his family after his death.

More than sixty vessels were launched from his North Harpswell-Brunswick yard, and were without exception, it was reported, all fine examples of careful and expert craftsmanship. The Pennells, Skolfields, and other shipbuilders tended to name their vessels after themselves or members of their families. This practice continues today among owners of boats of all sizes everywhere.

George was a grandson of Thomas Skolfield, who came to Boston from Dublin, in 1730, with sister Susan and the Orrs, John, Clement, Joseph, and Mary. Tom taught Latin in Boston, where he married Mary Orr in 1736. Three years later they came to Brunswick to be followed by the Orr brothers in 1742. (John had married Susan Skolfield.)

Tom Skolfield became a leading citizen of the young town, serving as a selectman for twenty-three years. He and Mary had a large family from whom all the later Skolfields were descended. Clement and Joseph Orr, likewise the ancestors of all of their name in Maine, settled in 1748 on the island that was later named for them.

The Skolfields, indeed—what a fine showing they were to make. Among at least twenty-five Skolfield captains were five Capt. Toms (three of whom built ships as well), and three Capt. Sams. Today it is all but impossible in some instances to identify each, the periods of their careers overlapping or the dates missing.

Among other large seafaring families were those of Alexander, Dunning, Curtiss, Johnson, Orr, Sinnett, Snow, and Stover—names that conjure up memories even today in Harpswell and Brunswick. But names, however often repeated, have no meaning in themselves. Here they stand for the collective nautical achievements of their families, for the most part. A few sketchy individual portraits are possible, even though we cannot describe either their physical appearance or their character in any detail. Little of that is necessary anyway, as the important thing is what they did, where they did it, and when. That, in itself, is what they were all about, and why they are playing their roles in this salty scenario.

Walter Meryman of Harpswell was the first settler of Birch Island. (1740, or soon thereafter.) His descendants, through sons Thomas, Hugh, Walter, James, and Michael, included a large number of the adventuresome who went West or followed the sea. No less than fifty Meryman sea captains sailed out of Maine ports—all of whom, ironically, were descended from this man who had been kidnapped in the port of Dublin, Ireland, and forcibly brought aboard ship to America.

Meryman was a Scots-Irishman, whose family name dated centuries back to medieval England. Even so, by the early 1800s many in his family were spelling their name Merryman or Merriman. The early Mainers were nothing if not independent, and from the time of the Revolution in particular had no use for Europe, its customs or traditions. They were so caught up in their new land and their own progress in it that they gave little or no thought to their own ethnic heritage. To all intents and purposes it was as though they had been cut out of whole cloth for this one time and place.

Attitudes today, in Maine as elsewhere, have broadened considerably. (Or been stretched, as some might say.) As part of the general relaxing of long held traditions, surnames are often changed completely. While no one can deny the right of any individual to be called by whatever name he chooses, this unsettling and continuing practice is proving unfortunate for people interested in trying to find and build upon family roots in both this country and in the lands of their ancestors.

Nothing eases the strict provincialism of any place as effectively as contact with the people and customs of other lands. Brunswick-Harpswell's young men had gone to sea and sailed to foreign countries, and it was only a matter of time before some understanding of the world and its people began to relax certain local prejudices. But Maine is still Maine today, and even the great influx of tourism has not entirely removed a cautious wariness—not so much distrust as a natural reticence and desire for privacy that has always been characteristic of some New Englanders. Outsiders consider this one of the charms of the area, finding it rather more humorous than harsh. No doubt some of this is cultivated especially for tourist consumption—all in the spirit of Down East neighborliness.

* * * *

The Pennell story rates telling in some detail, more perhaps than that of any family in the area during the sailing ship years. We will not do so here, but will fill in a few of the more obvious gaps. Their story began early on in Brunswick when the little town had a scattering of small shipyards and before the Pennells dominated the scene. Many sea captains established their reputations on the smaller craft of the period before joining the Pennell fleet later on.

The same can be said of master carpenters who had learned their trade well before accepting the challenge of larger vessels and an accelerated work pace. But the Pennell family itself was so large that, for several generations, they not only produced shipwrights for their own yard but for others as well in Brunswick and Harpswell.

Among the coastal clans they ranked at or close to the top in all phases of the building and the sailing of ships. They could not compete with the Merymans in sea captains—some of whom commanded Pennell ships—and the Skolfield family vied with them on all levels. In the end, though, it is Pennellville that is best remembered today when one thinks of the sailing ship era in Brunswick and vicinity.

By the sheer force of numbers they built a little empire on the shores of Casco Bay, and maintained it until the decreasing demand for their product no longer made continuance profitable. In the process they contributed mightily to the prosperity of Brunswick, and gave the town a firm base upon which other business enterprises were developed over the years. What they got out of it for themselves was obviously well deserved. In a larger sense, the Pennell accomplishments had been a great boost for Maine as a whole and for the sailing ship era in this country.

By the mid-nineteenth century, Great Chebeague Island had gained considerable fame along the coast for the large fleet of stone sloops and schooners that were operated by the Hamilton family of that large Casco Bay island. They were broad beamed vessels built especially to carry rock, stone, and granite slabs from Rockland to ports on the east coast. The Hamiltons, descendants of Ambrose Hamilton, who settled on the island in 1760, were related through marriage to several Harpswell families.

While it is easy enough to identify the families of Brunswick and Harpswell who made the greatest impression during Maine's day in the nautical sun, there were scores of others who worked as hard, both for themselves and for the common good. As it has always been, the majority of citizens did their jobs, lived out their lives, and were then quickly forgotten in the overall picture of their time and place. The world simply moves too fast to take note of all who deserve some mention in the human scheme of things, and though we are concerned only with a few scant miles of Maine coast and the few thousand people who lived there in a limited period of time, it would be impossible to attempt more than a very general recognition of their presence and accomplishments.

This in no way detracts from the families and persons we have mentioned. On the contrary, the fact that they stood out somewhat, for various reasons, serves to further indicate their right to some measure of justifiable pride. They should no more be forgotten than the great clipper ships should be allowed to pass into history unsung and sunken without a trace.

While it would be somewhat unfair, and a bit tedious as well, were we to attempt to name all known vessels and masters out of this one small section on the Maine coast, there would be a distinct void in this story were we not to give attention to some of the better known or best recorded sea captains of Harpswell and Brunswick. The scope of their work reached far beyond their home ports, or even this land as a whole, Again, it is what they represent fully as much as what they did that makes them important, not only to our story but to the entire history of the sailing ship years. We have seen this earlier, and it bears repeating at this time.

Our selections were not lightly made, and hopefully will not appear in any way provincial—not an easy task considering the limited area we are covering. So we shall name a few names in the next two chapters, and personalize, to some degree, the larger story of ships and men. For some who, perhaps, should have as clearly rated mention, let their spirits remain at ease. They are not forgotten, and hopefully their turn will come and they, too, will emerge to be recalled for the part they played in the glory days of sail.

Anonymous

Men without faces,
Men without names,
Marched in the mud
Of a dozen wars,
Seeded this land
Three thousand miles,
And nobody knows
Who they were.

Men without faces,
Men without names,
Serve this land
As their fathers did,
Asking nothing
For all they give,
And nobody knows
Who they are.

VII
CAPT. JACOB AND CAPT. SAM

"They've sailed the seas from Hong Kong to Gibraltar,
On plain and hill they have reared home and altar,
Typhoon and blizzard never made them falter;
Some clans get fresh, our clan is growing salter."

These hearty lines by the Rev. C.N. Sinnett from an introduction to his 1905 genealogy of the Merymans could have as well applied to other families in Brunswick and Harpswell during the nineteenth century. Horizons were being extended both on land and sea, and large families were the order of the day. And as a general rule the biggest families were the most successful, having their own homegrown talent and workforce.

   The closeness of the families in Harpswell was no more evident there than it was in all the Maine settlements at that time. In the beginning people kept together as much or as well as they could simply for survival. Even so, until past the mid-eighteenth century, Indian raids were possible anywhere and at any time. Fortunately the settlers had much in common aside from their obvious needs, and although they often lived some distance from their nearest neighbors, they were far from isolated.

   Once a settlement became established, for instance, a church was built. All citizens were not only expected to attend regularly but came under various forms of rude attention if they failed to do so. Those who came from Massachusetts would have found scarcely greater tolerance in their adopted province—at least in the earlier decades—than they had known in the Puritan Bay State. For most of them, though, it had always been an accepted way of life.

The roles of wives and mothers were surely as important at this time as those of the pioneer women who played such a vital part in the settlement of the West. Although theirs was a largely anonymous contribution, as nearly all the efforts of women were until well into the twentieth century, the sea captains of those days relied upon their support at home which, it would seem, was often well above and beyond the call of duty.

Nor was it too unusual to find a captain's wife making voyages with her husband, and on occasion being of practical assistance as well. And the daughters of shipmasters were often influential in fostering the nautical careers of their husbands and sons.

One of the more successful shipmasters, Capt. Jacob Meryman (1807-1863), gained his first opportunities through his mother's family. He was the only son of John (a ship carpenter son of Birch Island Hugh) and Molly Skolfield, and it was the Skolfield connection that inspired his seafaring ambitions. While still a boy he came under the influence of his uncle, Capt. John Orr Skolfield. It must have worked well for him, for by the time of his marriage to Susan Sumner Baker of Portland in 1833, Meryman had become a well-established shipmaster. The following year he took command of the newly launched brig *Frances*, built by another uncle, Jacob Skolfield, at Mere Point.

In 1836, Capt. William Stanwood, also a Mere Point shipbuilder, completed the 548-ton ship *Scotland*. She was put into service for the Red Star Line of New York, and for the next eight or nine years Capt. Jacob was her master. A packet ship, she sailed regularly between New York and Liverpool, and later out of Boston and New Orleans for the Despatch Line. This was, as told in a previous chapter, extremely demanding duty for a shipmaster, as schedules were expected to be kept and responsibility for speed as well as safety rested entirely upon the captain. An average year's run between New York and Liverpool was four round trips, for which the captain would receive about $20,000 from his share of passenger, freight, and mail revenue—very large money at the time.

Capt. Jacob was born on Birch Island, the fourth generation of his family to call it home. During his lifetime, this once busy and productive little island was slowly abandoned by its inhabitants. While a fine place to live, Birch Island was too small to provide opportunities for its young people. As they left so did the older folk, rather than remain apart from their families.

Capt. Jacob A. Meryman (1807-1863)

Most of those who left went to mainland Harpswell or Brunswick although some were reputed to have headed for the gold fields of California. Capt. Jacob had his own fortune to seek—eastward to the sea.

A sturdily built and stern man, Capt. Jacob Meryman was a classic example of a sea captain suited to his occupation under the hardy conditions of the period. (Packet ship crews—often referred to as "packet rats"—were a rather rough lot, as their hard and dangerous work would indicate they might well be.)

But the packet captain had to be far more than a commanding and capable figure pacing the quarterdeck. Out of deference to his passengers, many of whom were persons of some renown or importance, he was also required to present a more social side. So he played the part of the genial host when not actually attending to his ship duties, leaving virtually no time for rest or sleep while at sea.

Many a clipper or packet captain found it extremely difficult to cater to passengers, whom he more or less regarded as a necessary evil. Considering the stress inherent in his position, almost intolerable during severely heavy weather, it can be seen that any intrusion into his duty time would have been provoking, to say the least.

Rapport with the paying passengers was an essential part of his job under any circumstances, however, so it is obvious that Capt. Jacob and other successful packet commanders had to be men of some patience and self-control, at least pleasant conversationalists, and with an appearance that would have inspired some confidence in passengers who, during hectic and dangerous crossings, may have been certain that they would never see land again.

It was a young man's game which, with its other requirements, mainly favored men in their thirties. By 1845, Capt. Jacob decided that he had reached the point of change. The packet routine had served his purpose, having further enhanced his firm reputation while providing some financial security. So he returned home to his family, turning over his command to another skipper. As luck would have it—if such it was—the *Scotland*, under her new captain, was lost in January 1846, on Arklow Bank, Ireland.

Capt. Jacob was not long between ships. George Skolfield, in 1847, launched the 728-ton ship *Brandywine*. With young Sam Skolfield aboard as mate—perhaps as a condition of Capt. Jacob becoming her master—the *Brandywine* sailed for several years in trade with China and

Capt. J. Walter Meryman [1837-1866]
As U.S. Navy ensign.

the East Indies. Although we know it could not have been so, this must have seemed almost relaxing to the Captain after the frantic packet ship years.

Actually it merely exchanged one set of dangers for others. Indian Ocean hurricanes and typhoons were famous for their size and ferocity, and voyages to the Orient were long and trying. The alternate Pacific route was also long, and involved rounding tricky Cape Horn. But the Captain had the ability and experience, and in 1849 he felt confident enough to take his twelve-year-old son, Walter, aboard on a China trip.

When Sam Skolfield became captain of the clipper *Rising Sun* in 1856, Walter served as mate, as Capt. Sam had for the lad's father only a few years before. This sort of interrelationship was fairly common aboard Maine ships, and usually worked out to the advantage of all concerned.

Oddly enough, the ultimate fate of the *Brandywine* was nearly identical to that of Capt. Jacob's former command, the *Scotland*. In January 1861, she also went down off the Irish coast, near Carnsore Point, Wexford—less than fifty miles south of the spot where the *Scotland* had foundered fifteen years before. Perhaps the ghost of the Captain's Irish great-granddad had been taking a terrible revenge for having been uprooted from his homeland more than a century earlier and pressed into colonial servitude—making certain, of course, that his seagoing descendant had long since left the doomed ships.

Retiring from the sea after twenty-five years as a shipmaster, Capt. Jacob remained in Portland only a short time before moving to Massachusetts with his wife, two sons, and two daughters. There the captain tended to his maritime investments—endangered now by the outbreak of the Civil War—and, living near Boston, kept an active interest in the doings at the port. It was doubtless discouraging to him to find the erstwhile bustling harbor reduced to war status, and the recently busy McKay yards no longer building the beautiful clippers that he, of all men, would have appreciated. He was concerned, too, for the future career of his seafaring son.

It was Capt. Walter now, since becoming a shipmaster on the *Rising Sun* at the age of twenty-one. But the move from Maine was soon followed by the rumblings from the South, and the young man made no secret of his feelings on the hot issue of human slavery. Late in 1861 he enlisted in the Union Navy, serving throughout the Civil War as an officer on various fighting craft in southern waters, seeing much action. In his brief career, Walter's service spanned the short but significant gap between the clipper ship [*Rising Sun*] and the ironclad monitor [*Suncook*].

I did not have the good fortune to know my grandfather—but then, neither did my father. Capt. Walter died in 1866, and in a series of strange coincidences, his younger brother, Richard, also died, at a rather early age, both brothers leaving widows who gave birth to sons several months later—their only children.

Capt. Sam Skolfield (1827-1916) was one of the most noted shipmasters out of Casco Bay, and he became a very popular figure during his long career. As did Capt. Jacob Meryman, Capt. Sam enjoyed early advantages through his family connections. This was also true of many other sea captains, however, and few of them reached a status close to that which he attained in his career.

Capt. Sam's first command was the ship *Dublin*, in 1850, followed by the *Roger Stewart* in 1852. Meanwhile, George Skolfield was making plans to build the first clipper in the Brunswick-Harpswell area, not realizing at the time that it would be the only clipper ever to be built there. In 1855 she was completed, a beautiful and expertly crafted vessel of 1,375 tons, measuring 207' x 39' x 27'. She was named *Rising Sun*, and Capt. Sam was designated as her first skipper. He made successful voyages with her to Europe and Australia (1856-58), but as one of Master George's top captains there were other new ships that also required his expertise on their initial voyages. Capt. Sam's reputation was already well established, his seamanship known from Maine to New York, and as surely in whatever ports his ships dropped anchor.

For more than thirty years Capt. Sam remained an active shipmaster, almost exclusively on Skolfield built ships, although he could have sailed for any line or owner anywhere along the coast had he so chosen. He is still best remembered in Brunswick and Harpswell as the first commander of the *Rising Sun*, although he had many other ships during the next two decades.

One of his later ships was the *Sam Skolfield*, which he took out for her maiden voyage in 1875. Years later—in November 1883—she was lost in a hurricane. The Skolfields were not overly dismayed, having gone that route more than a few times before. And there was a new ship of comparable size that their yards were about to launch. It was promptly named the *Sam Skolfield II*.

It was about this time that Capt. Sam finally packed it in and turned over his long time duties to younger aspirants, although by now there was not that much left to aspire to, as the sailing ship era was rapidly drawing nearer to its inevitable conclusion. There would be sailing vessels of one sort or another along the coast for many years yet but the glory days were gone and irretrievable. In 1902, the *Sam Skolfield II* was sold to outside interests, and her full-length figurehead, carved to represent Capt. Sam, was removed.

For some reason, it got out of the hands of the Skolfields, and it was discovered by chance some years later serving as someone's lawn decoration in Winthrop, Massachusetts. This indignity was rectified in an appropriate manner soon thereafter when it was hung over the entrance to the Sailor's Haven in Charlestown, Massachusetts, where it remained for a good many years as an object of curiosity—and perhaps some respect—on the part of sailors and passers-by.

Capt. Sam has a long life in retirement as he had enjoyed at sea. There was much to remember, and to recall for anyone interested. It is unfortunate that he, in common with most retired sea captains, did not write down some of his recollections and adventures. Perhaps he felt, as many of his peers probably did as well, that his experiences belonged to him alone and ought to die with him. If he believed in immortality, it was not to be confused with tales that would outlive him, and in all likelihood become distorted, perhaps grossly, over the years.

Nothing more was needed during the years when retired sailing ship captains and sailors were alive than a few able and honest chronologists and historians who could have faithfully recorded the highlights, at least, in the careers of this hardy and dying breed of men. If there were any such around at the time it is not evident today. There may be some true tales in private hands, or hidden in dust-covered books somewhere, but the public domain reveals little other than a few oft-repeated yarns of largely questionable fact.

At the height of his career, Capt. Sam Skolfield was a rather elegant picture-book sea captain—dark haired and with a flowing mustache and invariably garbed in a manner befitting his stature in his profession. And a profession it was, in the heyday of sail. Unlike many Maine shipmasters, he was not averse to promoting himself as a part of his inducement to skippers and passengers to use the vessels he commanded. While hardly the only captain to feature personality as a selling point, Capt. Sam's success and longevity were due mainly to his ability on duty, any lack of which no amount of "show biz" could have hidden for a single voyage. Despite the absence of detail concerning his career his record as known stands today as eloquent testimony to that unquestioned ability.

* * * *

Capt. Jacob and Capt. Sam were but two shipmasters worthy of the name out of dozens from this one small section of the Maine coast. They represented, however, as well as any others could have, two entirely different styles of performance as sea captains.

Not only were they quite unlike in personality, but more importantly they sailed in different periods and under conditions that were constantly changing. Capt. Jacob was a hardnosed driver at a time when such tactics were necessary for survival, much less any degree of success. Capt. Sam, twenty years younger than his former mentor, could afford the luxury of being a more moderate leader. Yet both were very able, and equally successful. Between them, they logged at least fifty-five years as shipmasters during the peak period of American sailing ships. Others did as well, certainly, but there were few better along the entire eastern seaboard.

At this late date it would be all but impossible to name the leading clipper or packet captains, much less rate them for skill and longevity. A few names come to mind—Capts. Nat Palmer, Lauchlan McKay, Robert Waterman—but there were many, and it would be grossly unfair to try to rank them. Whatever information could be obtained today through research would be questionable, as there would be no sure way to check either accuracy or completeness.

Carl Cutler's 1930 classic, *Greyhounds of the Sea*, offers a good example. It was easily the most complete and painstakingly compiled history of the clipper ships ever written. Yet it lists the *Rising Sun* and names Capt. Orr as her first commander. It is well known in Harpswell that Sam Skolfield held that honor and that Capt. Harmon Orr did not take over this vessel until the 1860s. A small point, perhaps, but indicative of just how difficult it is to accumulate accurate data from often conflicting or incomplete sources many decades after the fact, beyond even the time-fogged memories of persons who had lived throughout the period.

Such maritime history as exists of Brunswick-Harpswell has been obtained largely from records of families involved at the time. This does not escape, either, the dual pitfalls of inaccuracy and omission. Enough verifiable fact does come through, however, to indicate that had there ever been established a Maine Hall of Fame for sea captains, these two towns would surely have been represented. The following chapter of necessarily brief sketches includes several of those who would almost certainly have been candidates for such honors.

Maine Ancestor

Beside the road
In a churchyard,
A sliver of slate
Marks his name and years.

Winters have kept
A place for him,
Where summer strangers
Pass too quick for tears.

VIII
THE TEAM ROSTER

Were this indeed the roster of an athletic team it would list those performers whose careers spanned many active years, while others would attain a peak of excellence only briefly, failing short due to injury or other causes. Such variation is similar in many lines of endeavor, and sea captains were no exception. On the contrary, because of the high incident of death, accident, and illness at sea in the days of sail, the average career of a shipmaster was relatively short. Aside from that, there was always the domestic factor. Most sea captains were married, and comparatively few wives sailed with their husbands, even occasionally. Many captains left the sea sooner than they might have otherwise because of their wives and families, absence for long periods of time at sea being usually more difficult for those at home than for the captains themselves.

The sailing ship was a most jealous mistress, and fortunate was the captain who could resolve and reconcile the demands of his career and his home for as long as he deemed necessary. Except for those whose time at sea may have seemed more of a blessing than a hardship for their spouses, one would have to sympathize with, and have admiration for, the captains' wives waiting at home. "Widows' Walks" atop some of their houses were not merely decorative, and too often they proved to be aptly named.

Maine sea captains were a particular breed of men, both because of their family background and because they were under somewhat less pressure than those who sailed for large firms out of Boston, New York, and other major ports. The Maine shipmasters were "family," interrelated and similar in many respects, yet there was a certain rivalry between them both on a personal level and as representatives of competing owners. Capt. Jacob Meryman and a few others out of Maine had long periods of "big time" sailing before returning home for a final fling with local ships prior to retirement. Because they were Mainers, however, comparatively few of the hundreds who sailed from the state's ports received the recognition that was accorded many of the clipper and packet captains out of New York and Boston or, in the earlier days, out of Salem and Newburyport with their smaller ships in the China trade.

Maine's late start in the world market had something to do with this, too. By that time the glamour of the whole thing had worn off somewhat, and only the best-known ships and their captains were given much attention.

Sobriety, in the dangerous day of sail, was necessary while a ship was at sea. For the Maine captains, many of whom were teetotalers, it was never a problem. If some of them enjoyed a grog or two while laying over in a foreign port, or kept a jug in their sea chest to warm themselves after a hard, cold trick on duty during a winter storm, it would have passed unnoticed. Seamen have not, on the whole, been noted for alcoholic abstinence, as everyone knows. Nor could Maine sailors, in spite of their usually sober upbringing, have completely ignored West Indies rum or some of the more exotic liquids available in other ports of call. We do not find references to drinking in records of the time, however, and can only conclude that it never became an issue aboard Maine sailing ships.

Any Maine sailing ship buff today will recognize at least some of the captains and seafaring families we mention here, and perhaps that is enough in view of the great numbers who were in the business locally during the state's "century of glory." Some might recall a few of the real old timers in the Harpswell area; captains like Jesse Snow, David Douglass, Ebenezer Woodward, Joshua Bishop, Jeremiah Webber, Henry Totman, John and Richard Pinkham, Isaac Rich, David

Doughty, Jacob Blake, Elisha Ribber, Robert McManus, and Coan Jordan, to name but a handful who come to mind. The names of some ships may be more recognizable than their captains or owners, but as a majority of the vessels were named after persons it might only be confusing to list them here.

It will be noted that the early captains commanded smaller vessels, or the best available in their time, accounting for the preponderance of sloops, brigs, and small schooners for the years prior to 1830. In Maine, in fact, even the larger shipyards did not turn to vessels of 1,000 tons or more until the 1850s. The comparatively light craft the early skippers handled were a challenge in themselves, and required at least as much skill to sail and keep afloat in heavy weather as any that sailed the oceans during the clipper ship days.

Many sailing ships, during their lifetime, served a number of different owners and captains. More than a few shipmasters commanded a dozen or more vessels over the course of their careers as well.

As we have observed, the deplorable lack of records makes it impossible today to list all of the ships that should be credited to the deep-water captains—and in some instances there are none that we can name, although we do know that the captains were active for many years and were quite successful.

The relatively small area encompassed by the towns of Brunswick and Harpswell saw hundreds of ships and masters during the era of sail, and it is not surprising that little remains of the hasty records kept a century or two ago. That busy and productive period was concerned with neither the past nor future, and, considering the success they made of it, we cannot fault the shipbuilders and owners for any lack of foresight they may have had regarding the maintenance and preservation of their records. Had they known at the time that the whole business would come to a screeching halt as quickly as it did they may have been more careful to save every scrap of tangible evidence of their accomplishments.

The following sea captains, mostly out of Harpswell, are a representative few, including some of the unlucky ones. As is the case whenever choice is involved, it cannot satisfy all who may be concerned. Nor is this an apology in any way. We may be quite sure that not one of the shipmasters named here would ever have explained a single decision or command of his while aboard ship, come hell or high water. That is one of the reasons they are listed here.

CAPT. JOHN SNOW [1768-1822]
Best known of the earlier Snow captains—there were at least a dozen in the family that we can trace—Capt. John is recorded as master of the schooner *Lady Washington*, brigantine *Polly*, schooner *Elizabeth*, and the schooner *Ocean*.

CAPT. DAVID CURTISS [1784-1860]
This prominent Harpswell family gave about ten sea captains to the local roster, including Capt. Angier (1816-1875), Capt. Peleg (1818-1879), and several who were lost at sea. Namesake of the Curtiss who came to Harpswell from Puritan Massachusetts in 1744, Capt. David is listed as master of the schooner *Morning Star* and the sloop *Mary Jane*.

CAPT. JAMES MERYMAN [1787-1876]
The lifetime of Capt. Meryman spanned nearly the entire "glory era" of Maine sailing ships, and while he contributed toward its success he is most noted as the father of four very able shipmaster sons: Capt. Paul (1820-1893), Capt. Hutson (1822-1867), Capt. Henry (1829-1868), and the oldest, Capt. Jeremiah, who sailed mainly for the Pennells on such vessels as the schooner *Grandilla*, bark *Nettie Merryman*, brig *John R. Dow*, and the brig *Galveston*.

CAPT. JOSEPH MERRIMAN [1788-1834]
One of the trader captains, he spent many years on the West Indies run, continuing to do so after moving to Hartford, Connecticut, in 1826. He made one trip too many, however. While en route to British Guiana in 1834 he was lost at sea with the brig *Eight Sons*. (Perhaps an early tangle with the Bermuda Triangle.)

CAPT. CLEMENT MARTIN [1789-1869]
Son of Capt. Matthew Martin, and generally ranked as the best shipmaster of his family. Among the ships he sailed in a busy career were the schooner *Abigail*, brig *Maine*, schooner *Susanna*, brig *Mentor*, brig *Amazon*, and the bark *Clement*.

CAPT. JAMES SINNETT [1790-1881]
One of the most warmly regarded of men, Capt. Sinnett was a long lived shipmaster out of Bailey Island who extended his interests by founding an entire family of captains—eleven, to be exact, including

three sons; Capt. David (1813-1888), Capt. Hugh (1814-1907), and Capt. William (1827-1894).

CAPT. CLEMENT SKOLFIELD [1803-1878]
Son of one of the Capt. Toms and a nephew of Master George, Capt. Skolfield had a fine career in his own right. Among the vessels he commanded were the brig *George*, ship *Washington*, brig *Alcencus*, and the ship *John Dunlap*.

CAPT. NORTON STOVER [1812-1898]
Son of Capt. Joshua, Norton Stover was a prominent citizen of Harpswell, owning one of the larger shipyards in town. He spent a good deal of time at sea earlier in life. Among the ships he commanded; the brig *Matanzas*, bark *Panama*, sloop *Excursion*, and the brig *Lydia Stover*.

CAPT. THOMAS ALEXANDER [1813-1858]
One of a dozen or more captains in this early Brunswick-Harpswell family, Capt. Alexander was struck down, as were so many seafarers, by yellow fever. While in command of the ship Scioto he died of this often-fatal ailment in New Orleans on August 3, 1858.

CAPT. SINNETT ORR [1817-1897]
The Orr captains hailed mostly from Bailey and Orr's Islands, around fifteen of them that we find recorded. Among the ships of Capt. Orr were the brig *Sea Bird* and the schooner *Mary H. Lewis*. He had one shipmaster son, Capt. James L. Orr (1846-1906).

CAPT. ALCOT MERRIMAN [1822-1865]
A prominent member of a large seafaring family, Capt. Merriman was master of the brig *William H. Parks*, among others. He was better known as a Harpswell shipbuilder, and was a selectman of the town at the time of his rather early death. The yard continued to operate under his nephew, Paul Merriman, for some years thereafter.

CAPT. ABIJAH STOVER [1823-1887]
One of the most able shipmasters out of Maine, Capt. 'Bijah spent nearly all of his adult life at sea. Son of Capt. Johnson Stover, he was the best known of about twenty Stover captains. He was still sailing the briny deep among skippers less than half his age when most of those

whose careers had started with his were ashore and doing nothing more strenuous than counting their grandchildren. Among Capt. 'Bijah's ships were the bark *Mary Ellen* (named for his wife), ship *Harpswell*, bark *Norton Stover*, bark *Clara Eaton*, and the bark *Daring*. This beloved captain is one who would surely be a candidate for our mythical Hall of Fame.

CAPT. ISAAC LINCOLN SKOLFIELD [1824-1898]
It is no simple matter to select just a few Skolfield captains—nor choose among the many other large seafaring families. Capt. "Linc" was particularly capable, however, and was shown as the master of the ship *John Dunlap* and the ship *Lydia Skolfield*, among others. (The *Lydia Skolfield* sailed for more than thirty years, and was one of the best of the famous downeasters.)

CAPT. ALFRED HAYDEN MERRYMAN [1825-1886]
Able shipmaster for about twenty years, Capt. Merryman later became a Brunswick banker. He sailed for the Pennells during his career at sea, and the ship *Oakland* was built for him after his former command, the ship *Ocean Home*, was cut down in the English Channel by a large New York packet ship. He was the brother of Capt. Benjamin Merryman, also of Brunswick. Among their local peers at the time were such other notable captains as William Woodside, and the brothers John D. and James H. Pennell.

CAPT. WALTER MERRIMAN [1835-1893]
Son of Capt. Shubal (1806-1898), and brother of Capt. Angier Merriman. Before the age of twenty-one, Capt. Merriman became master of the bark *Andes*. Among his later ships were the brigantine *Angier H. Curtiss* and the bark Isaac Lincoln. Aboard the latter in 1869, nearing the Pacific port of Calleo, Peru, he and his wife Lavina became parents of a baby boy.

CAPT. JOHN MERRYMAN [1836-1886]
One of the relatively few bachelor captains, and rated as one of the best in his time, Capt. Merryman died of fever as far from home as he could have gotten, on the coast of China. Two of his brothers were also able masters. One of them, Capt. David (1839-1892), became a dentist ashore after twenty years at sea. Something to consider—a sea

captain dentist before the day of painless dentistry!

CAPT. ALFRED DUNNING [1844-1919]
Perhaps it is fitting that we conclude our all too brief list of sketches with one of about fourteen Dunning shipmasters, as this early family contributed greatly in getting things moving, ship-wise and otherwise. Capt. Dunning did most of his sailing for Master George Skolfield, commanding several of the larger vessels owned by the sagacious shipbuilder. And he was also a survivor of the ill-fated ship *Sam Dunning* in 1865, while serving as third mate.

* * * *

Obviously, a well-informed descendant of any shipbuilding or seafaring family in Brunswick-Harpswell might add much more to the preceding sketches. For our part, though, it serves the purpose. Perhaps this will inspire someone to write a book about his seagoing ancestors. From what we have learned about their times and activities, it could be most interesting and colorful.

No attempt has been made here to put together a list of the best-rated captains from this area. Some are included, of course, and others may have been added had more information about them been available. (Including several Pennell shipmasters.) Captains Edmund Wilson (1822-1913) and James Dyer (1834-1914), although not of the larger seafaring families, made their own marks and would be welcomed on any "team" of able shipmasters. The Wilsons, one of the first families in the region (Topsham, 1719), later turned out a few sea captains and shipbuilders in Harpswell.)

So much for names, which do not mean all that much today except to those related to, or familiar with, them. Collectively, however, they represent a hardy group of men who accomplished a very dangerous job of work under often adverse conditions and with notable success. As such, they richly merit individual recognition.

The use of the word "team" as applied to the captains is purely a convenience, of course. The same term used in describing the shipyards of the time would have been much more appropriate. From their owners and master carpenters down to their most menial laborers, shipyards were run with a high degree of cooperative skill. Anything less would have been fatal to their business in the competitive and demanding field of shipbuilding, whether their yards were large or small. Teamwork was fully as important to a successful operation as the experience and the skills of the personnel. In this respect the old shipyards were no different from well run businesses and industries today.

The shipyards of Maine, operated often by large family units, experienced little difficulty in maintaining the high morale necessary to turn out a quality product. The example of the Skolfield yards has been cited. Their business was different, however, in one notable respect from other large shipyards in the Brunswick-Harpswell area. Their ships were, for the most part, not built to sell to others but to be sailed for, and by, members or relatives of their own family. Even the redoubtable Pennells could not match the Skolfield "closed shop" operation, wherein owners, builders, and captains, in one way or another, all shared in the business.

Years ago, while living for a time in Portland, I came across a city directory for the year 1844. Opposite the names of persons residing in the city their occupations were listed. I could not begin to count the great numbers of shipmasters, on page after page, and I realized that Brunswick and other towns along the coast would also, at the time, have had an equally high ratio of sea captains among their citizens.

This continued to be true until the outbreak of the Civil War, diminishing slowly thereafter for the remainder of the century in much the same manner that small farmers all over the country were forced to give in to changing conditions decades later. The advent of steam power, which spelled doom for the sailing shipmaster, was but a prelude to the industrial revolution and mechanization that was soon to engulf the smaller farmer and businessman. Shipbuilders and sea captains were by no means the sole victims of the progress they had worked so hard to achieve, which was small comfort to them, to be sure. What they did accomplish in such impressive numbers, however, is beyond our wish today to either forget or fail to appreciate.

History dwells at great length upon violence of one sort or another, as change is usually accompanied by such, in war or peace, In the long run, however, it is the work of the builder, rather than the destroyer, that creates and sustains a society in any land at any time. Yet, as we have seen in the careers of the sea captains, building can involve great risk and challenge and be in no way dull or routine.

Shipmasters and their blood brothers, the pioneers of the old West, were the most rugged and fearless of men. Their contributions to this country stand out in sharp contrast, as an extreme example, to those of their contemporaries, the western gunslingers, whose exploits have always commanded far greater public and media attention. Nor can popular history be exempted from some criticism for its seeming priorities. For whatever reason anyone may choose otherwise, our pioneers on land or sea, as a breed of men, have been rarely equaled in the entire annals of mankind for sheer courage and for signal achievements of skill and daring. Theirs was no mere one on one confrontation. Man against the sea, certainly, involved the lives of many, and of their great ships as well.

Looking back upon the efforts and accomplishments of the sea captains can give us both hope and inspiration in our own lives and for the lives of generations yet to come—however different the world may be today. People are still people. The sailing ships may have gone, but the men who built and sailed them live on in ourselves—whether we are descended from them by blood or in spirit, for there are no racial or ethnic barriers anywhere, any time, to human character, courage, or ambition.

IX
THE LADIES, BLESS 'EM

Except for a paragraph of so there has been no mention thus far of the part women have taken in this story of ships and men. Their role was considerable, of course, and clearly mentions full attention. The large families in villages and towns along the Maine coast averaged as many daughters as sons, and they were surely as important to the growth of their communities as the men who farmed and fished, built the houses and ships, and sailed the seas. The endless chores wives and mothers performed daily to raise their families and keep them fed and clothed were arduous indeed; we need not go into detail here, for everyone is aware of what was involved in everyday rural living in the New England of the eighteenth and nineteenth centuries. We know, also, that women were the principal force in the establishment and maintenance of schools and churches—even though town officials and members of the clergy, whose names adorned documents founding them, were invariably male. The influence of women then was generally far more subtle than it is today, but we cannot see that it was any the less effective.

If family life was difficult in coastal regions it was even more demanding on the islands offshore. Yet these tiny settlements offered some measure of protection from Indian attack during the early decades of Maine's development. Birch Island, for example, favored with timber, arable land, and natural spring water, was settled mainly for reasons of safety. Walter and Betsey (Potter) Meryman raised their eight children there and were soon joined by other families until it became necessary to set up a school on the island.

Other islands in Casco Bay and along the coast were similarly settled at that time, and while island living may have been somewhat confining, especially in winter, there is little doubt that women found their days fully occupied with their work and families, with neighbors in sufficient numbers, at least, for some social contact. It was a life that required a good deal of getting used to for some. They were, though, far less lonely than their sisters who went West and settled the seemingly endless plains, often far out of sight of their nearest neighbor.

On the mainland, meanwhile, shipyards were springing up. Many of the men who worked in them kept family farms as well, small as farms are envisioned today, but large enough so that it meant their wives were left with chores to do outside in addition to their household duties while the men were at work. If sons were old enough to help it was some relief. As more and more of the young men left home to go to sea, women were again left with many of the routine chores, daughters as well as wives. Nor was marriage any solution for the young women, although their early training would serve them in good stead in homes of their own.

The mere fact of being women, however, in no way lessened the impact the ladies of the Harpswell area had upon either their families or their communities. They were, after all, equal partners of a hardy breed of men whom they often matched or exceeded at many levels of physical activity, and certainly in every other respect. Harpswell recorded the determination of one feisty Puritan lady, Hannah (Curtiss) Bailey who, with little help from her husband, ousted a somewhat rowdy old squatter, Will Black, from an island she coveted. But for her, Bailey Island might be known today as Will's Island. (We suspect that the place was named fully as much for her as for her husband, Deacon Timothy.)

Although Harpswell ships traded extensively for many years with ports in the West Indies it appears that their young sailors did not favor the native girls as far as marriage was concerned. If the feeling were there, getting the permission of the captain would have presented an obstacle difficult to overcome—not to mention the approval of family and neighbors back home. The women of coastal Maine were as proud and clannish a lot as their menfolk, and would scarcely have tolerated any intrusion into their way of life by a number of olive complexioned females from foreign shores. There were several rare exceptions over the years, but the good ladies of Harpswell and vicinity generally kept their men pretty much to themselves. Their only real competition came from the white-sailed ships that took many of their men away for long periods of time, and too often for all time.

As we have seen, there was never any lack of appreciation for female members of shipbuilding or seafaring families. Their vessels frequently bore the names of their wives or other lady relatives. Capt. Richard Merryman sailed for some time on the *Marcia Greenleaf*, named for his wife.

Although the captain died and his widow left for California with their two small children, the ship bearing her name continued to sail the seas under other masters for more than twenty years thereafter.

On several known occasions, a captain's wife, sailing with him, was responsible for getting their ship home after the captain was taken seriously ill aboard. Ship's mates were not always navigators—fortunately, at those times, the captain's mates were. Capt. Peleg Merriman and his wife, Clara, had such an experience aboard the bark *Ella* in the late 1800s. En route home from South America, both the captain and the mate came down with fever and took to their bunks. The second mate could handle the vessel, but did not know navigation. So Clara not only took care of her patients but, having learned how to navigate, guided their ship safely home to Portland as well.

Stories handed down from generation to generation as gospel truth may as we know, become distorted in some way over the years. The following, being short and simple, is most likely strictly factual.

Many long years ago, Abigail Eastman of Great Island was observing, one day, a debate among the men in her family on how best to get a freshly killed three hundred pound hog up to their house. Without a word the large and very strong woman picked up the heavy carcass, flung it over her shoulder, and quickly carried it up the yard and into the house. Nearly as quickly, or soon after the story got around, Abigail got married—to, it was reported, "a small man of great energy." This is the end of the tale as we know it. While we somehow get the feeling that it may have been only the beginning, it does clearly indicate, if nothing else, that the men of early Maine had a deep appreciation for true practical value—looking at it from the rather elemental standpoint of the period and region.

In spite of the hardships experienced during the earlier days in Maine, then as now wives very often outlived their husbands. But as families were both large and closely involved the elderly were cared for in a manner that is not too often observed today. They were proud people and quite self-sufficient. It was unthinkable to suggest that a family could not "do for themselves."

The closeness of the neighboring families was dramatically demonstrated quite often by the marriage of several brothers in one family to the sisters in another. Two or three generations of this sort of intermarriage was not uncommon, among some of the earlier families in particular. Nor was it unusual for cousins to marry each other, or for a niece to marry an uncle.

Although there were rather limited options for eligible young men and women in the small and scattered settlements, they generally made out quite well.

Maine women took at least as much pride in the accomplishments of their male relatives as did the men themselves. The larger and earlier families in each community became a sort of implied local aristocracy, and a family's name was its most treasured asset. There is little doubt that some daughters in those families would marry only the sons of equally "good name"—even though there were not too many candidates at times. But family pride went beyond marriage. Single ladies, either by choice or otherwise, were as proud of the families they were born into as were their married sisters.

As one generation followed another, whatever distinctions there may have been between families in any settlement or town became virtually non-existent because of the high incidence of intermarriage. The only difference that made to Yankee ladies, married or not, was that they now had several old families of equal standing to verify their solid New England heritage. To their credit, most Maine women kept this to themselves. Not only were there others of equally good old lineage around, but it was now becoming unfashionable to mention it at all, in view of the increasing numbers of ethnic minorities in the state. Today, for most part, the old family ladies of Maine leave the heritage stuff to their high society sisters in Boston and other centers of culture and dollar divinity.

In 1763, Thomas Meryman married Sarah, a daughter of Timothy

Bailey. That same year Tom built her a house on Bailey Island, which is still a private home today. As many men were carpenters out of necessity, this was a common practice at the time. Quite often a bride could expect a new house in which to begin her married life. Until more lavish houses were built, such as those at Pennellville, they were relatively simple one-story structures, although sturdy and roomy enough to contain growing families comfortably and well.

Harriet Beecher Stowe, in her 1862 book, *The Pearl of Orr's Island*, told a good deal about the way of life for women in the early and mid-nineteenth century along the Maine coast. Her novel was the first written about the area to become nationally known, although it was not so much appreciated by some of the local inhabitants at the time. Stowe's fine descriptions of coastal scenery and her word picture of sailing ships coming home to port is still considered effective writing today.

And in this century, Edna St. Vincent Millay, famed poetess, spent many summers on Ragged Island, south of Harpswell. Her work, however, did not reflect on the coastal scene to any extent, past or contemporary.

There were few career opportunities available to women in nineteenth century Maine, but this was true nearly everywhere in the country outside of the larger cities. Women who did not marry and needed to earn their own living did so in a rather modest fashion in a wide variety of jobs, mainly domestic. Some attained a good measure of satisfaction in teaching careers, a few becoming well known throughout the state. The New England spinster was a very special breed, highly independent and at least as resourceful as the men of her time. Many would doubtless have been heard from had opportunities existed for them in the business world or in the arts. There was little for them in Maine, and travel to other states, with perhaps a better chance to earn more and advance according to their ambitions, was also difficult and risky for women alone.

The vast majority of women, of course, were far too busy with their homes and families to undertake anything further for their own personal fulfillment. Their influence for good upon their husbands and children was their greatest and most lasting achievement throughout Maine's first two hundred years. The history of every Brunswick-Harpswell family is essentially the story of mothers, wives, and daughters who knit the sturdy fabric of their families into one great tapestry involving their entire community. Obviously this would have to be true for the success of any town of whatever size and location, and it was certainly so in any of the settlements on the coast of Maine. However we may stress the achievements of the male element, we cannot and should not for one moment fail to credit the women who, in the truest sense, made those successes not only possible but likely. For most women, accustomed as they were to the mores of their time, it as reward enough and personally satisfying.

Young women today, on the whole, find little to cheer about in viewing the hard working self-sacrifice of their female predecessors. They would not, for example, understand that men too, for most part, were equally hard working and selfless.

Had not both marriage partners shared their labor and responsibilities they could not have raised the large families so many of them brought into the world, young men and women who were very much needed in the rapidly expanding country. One has only to look through family genealogies of the time to find generation after generation of such large numbers of sons, daughters, and grandchildren that we can scarcely believe it possible, judging by the standards we have known in our own lifetime. We cannot fairly equate yesterday with today on this score, of course. Suffice it to say, our ancestral mothers took to their tasks and did them well.

It was not until well into the current century—after women had gotten the vote, the "flapper" era, and Valentino—that America suddenly discovered Sex. This remarkable revelation was immediately followed by gales of laughter from the rest of the world, and from a smattering of old ladies in Maine who recalled their salty forbears. A chunky blonde from Brooklyn quickly grasped the humor of the situation and proceeded to amass a fortune as an ever-obvious sex symbol in Hollywood. But the best was yet to come. Political emancipation and sexual awareness awakened women everywhere to bright new possibilities for their gender. After serving in the armed forces and on many hitherto male jobs during World War II, American women were encouraged to take themselves very seriously indeed. There was no more laughter. Women's liberation movements were started that would in a matter of two or three decades produce an entirely new concept of women's personal and professional lives.

Some of this had been foreseen by the poet Walt Whitman in his 1855 *Leaves of Grass*. Although he could not have imagined the extent to which it would lead, he had boldly declared the full equality of women. This had been, even in mid-nineteenth century, quite generally understood by many reasonable people, although not often admitted publicly.

Today some women find it demeaning to be referred to as such, preferring to be called simply "persons." This would surely have outraged our female ancestors, who had always thought themselves rather more distinctive than that. Most of them, in fact, neither felt nor acted in any way inferior to men. On the contrary, they believed strongly in the status of womanhood and in the subtle influence it gave them. Those who were at all intimidated by the sometimes illusionary male dominance of the time would, if living in today's world, be equally susceptible to it.

The point—if one is needed—is that a woman is a woman in any era, and has every right and reason to be proud of the fact.

The Harpswell of a century or two ago was much farther removed from the present time than the mere number of intervening years would appear to indicate. Whether or not the life style of that bygone day was more satisfying on the whole than that which we know today is a question that is largely unanswerable as it would involve many varied viewpoints and opinions. For certain, the demands of progress are great, and for everything gained, something of value must be sacrificed. As each passing era has learned, there is no way to either return to the past or to halt the inevitable progress of people or nations, whatever it may lead to over the long haul. Courses must be run, and each generation is in the race, willingly or otherwise.

Those who came before us had no other options either, although perhaps most of them wished for none as changes from one generation to another were less violent and demanding upon individuals, except, of course, in time of war. Women, bound as they were by the conventions of their day, adjusted to changing conditions rather better than many of the men, an ability they have always possessed to a remarkable degree. As they guided and held together their families and communities in New England's pioneer days, so they worked for their growth and progress during the sailing ship era. However different the lives of women may be today, however much they have gained and may yet attain, the ladies of old Harpswell need never have envied them. Their rest was well earned, and they will never be forgotten, either for what they were and represented or for all that they accomplished in their blessed time on earth.

In the 1800s America had all manner of ambitions, grand dreams of expansion and growth, and the means to attain them. The world of sailing ships had its own horizons, literally and figuratively. Our sea captains set out for them without having to be reminded of the worth and warmth of their ladies at home, as autocratic as they may have been while aboard ship. Wives and mothers suffered the long months, and sometimes years, of their absences. For some, it became almost unbearable.

It was a sea widow's lot, however, and few dared to complain, as it was the common fate of many. Today, understanding more of human need in all respects, we can more fully realize the depth of their fears and the extent of their patience. And we know, too, perhaps better than did the shipmasters themselves, how truly indispensable their women were to them and, indeed, to the entire era of the sailing ships.

X
AFTER THE FACT

Portrait in Salt

He had ice-blue splinters of steel for eyes,
And a face well weathered and tan,
And he fought the sea for lobsters
In days when it challenged a man.

Now and then, along the way,
He welcomed aboard a new son,
And all kept busy on boat or farm
And I know, for I was one.

He had ice-blue splinters of steel for eyes,
Belying the warmth inside,
And seven sons and eighty years
And love till the day he died.

From the foregoing chapters one might suppose that I had grown up knowing all about my father's seafaring ancestry and about Harpswell's part in the history of Maine. Not so. Until later in life I was almost entirely unaware of either. The reason for this is a story in itself, one that began as far back as 1864 in the residential Boston suburb of Chelsea.

Capt. Jacob's wife, Susan, who took perhaps excessive pride in being the daughter of a Sumner, the then prominent Massachusetts political family, had been most influential in getting the Captain to move to the Bay State. Following his death in 1863 her ambitions turned toward securing "proper" marriages for her children—meaning, of course, uniting with Boston families of some social and financial prominence. Her oldest son, Walter, was her first concern, and quickly became her sharpest disappointment. The erstwhile clipper captain, now a dashing young naval officer, had already fallen in love with the attractive and equally spirited daughter of a Boston engraver. No amount of persuasion could deter him. While home on a short leave in May 1864, he and Mary Swett were married.

But there was to be no happy ending for any of them. The war over, Walter returned home early in 1866. He was not well, and as we have previously noted, lived only a few months. Grief was now added to his mother's earlier woes, and it was far worse for Mary who was expecting her baby that summer. The two widows had one thing left in common aside from mutual sorrow—unrelenting pride. Walter's mother, having virtually disinherited him when he married against her wishes, would have nothing to do with either her son's widow or with the baby boy who arrived that July. Mary was equally adamant. Not only did she refuse to seek financial aid for herself or her son from her husband's family, but would not thereafter refer to them again. For years, or until her son was old enough to help, Mary survived mainly on her meager widow's war pension and by taking in sewing.

As my father grew up knowing little of his father's family it follows that I learned almost nothing of them either. When I finally looked into it later, and considered the sour turn of events following the family's move from Maine, I could not help but regret that they had ever left the Pine Tree State.

None of this ever seemed to concern my father—yet another Walter Meryman. An active outdoorsman all his life, he was a hunter and trapper in youth, spending several winters in the lower Florida

Everglades after the turn of the century. He became thereafter a long time lobsterman-farmer and storekeeper. In many respects he was a kind of throwback to earlier Maine ancestors, very much a responsible individualist. Had his father lived there is little doubt that he would have become the shipmaster he always gave the appearance of being. Following a short-lived earlier marriage, he met and later married Lily Cainey, a gentle English lass much younger than he. They settled down to a hard-working family life in the seacoast town of Winthrop, bordering Boston.

Of my father's seven sons—two of them by his first wife—only the oldest followed the sea. Born in 1898, Eugene enlisted in the U.S. Navy in 1918 for four years, and then graduated from maritime school. From that time until his retirement after forty-five years at sea, Eugene served as an officer on oil tankers, including much perilous duty during World War II. His entire sea career spanned nearly fifty years, a period of service that would have been totally inconceivable during the sailing ship era.

As early as the age of ten I went lobstering with my father, rowing the boat while he hauled his pots off Point Shirley or around outer Boston Harbor. There were many yacht clubs in the area, and all summer long sailboats cut their courses around us, beautiful symbols, we thought, of the leisurely and more affluent life. Being a large and busy family, we never considered ourselves in any way deprived or under-privileged—at least until the Great Depression of the 1930s.

While working in a shipyard at South Portland, Maine, during World War II, I became for the first time generally aware of Harpswell's seafaring history. Due to war service and subsequent events, it was many years before my next visit to Harpswell. Yet it was inevitable that I would return. One's homeland remains in the blood through many generations, whether one is aware of it or not. But, of course, no one has ever been born without deep roots into the past, and a long heritage that is as much a part of himself as the life he lives.

Ancestor worship—American style—has long been associated with the so-called WASP culture in New England, particularly in Boston. While, as we have seen, there may be some basis for a certain amount of pride in Yankee tradition, it is certainly no guarantee of present or future vigor or success. State of Mainers, on the whole, have never subscribed to what they regard as snobbishness or excessive glorification of the past, although they are well aware of their proud history and find a sort of quiet strength in that knowledge, because of their Down East independence, and perhaps because they do not associate themselves with the Massachusetts social hierarchy. Coast of Mainers have always seemed light years removed from the still influential Boston Brahmin caste. The fact is, however, that some of the Bay State fortunes were founded by astute Maine shipbuilders and sea captains of the 1800s.

There is a general distrust among old line folks in Maine of any place larger than Portland. I once met a man in that city who, in his obvious Down East accent, told of having been trapped in an elevator while visiting Boston. He made it sound as though it had been a high point in his life, and the only impression he had gotten of the old Hub. I gathered, however, that he had been greatly relieved to get back home, unscathed and uncorrupted by his association, however brief, with Boston. Perhaps he is still living today, quietly and confidently in Maine, telling again and again of his near disaster outside of his own domain. Perhaps, too, the story was a put-on for the benefit of a gullible tourist.

For many long months every year sailing boats of many types and sizes are seen along the coast, in and out of bays, harbors, and rivers, white or colored sails against the sea. The pure pleasure of sailboating is appreciated more today than ever, yet no one imagines himself—seriously, at any rate—a windjammer captain in the context of the clipper ship era. There could simply be no such comparison. Fun and games are quite different from often grim reality, and few of us are prepared today to handle the hardship and the risks that the old shipmasters faced daily. Life has its compensating challenges in other fields, but as far as the sea is concerned the greatest dangers are long past. Even so, men are lost at sea every year, and it cannot ever be taken lightly.

An example of this occurred as recently as August 1979, during international yacht races along the English Channel between the Isle of Wight and Fastnet Rock off Ireland's southern coast. More than three hundred sailing boats were caught in a sudden storm of near hurricane intensity, for which neither the light craft nor their crews were prepared or equipped. About thirty boats sank or were abandoned and at least fifteen men were lost. But for expert seamanship many more may have foundered. Although most of the craft were well constructed, they were built for speed and were neither large nor heavy enough to cope with ocean storm conditions. All but one American boat came through the ordeal in good order. (The United States has always been number one in yacht racing, despite increasingly stiff challenges from other nations.)

Today there is serious thought being given to building sailing ships for commercial use, due to the increasing high cost of energy. Such craft would still use engine power when necessary, operating by sail only under favorable wind conditions. This seeming reversal, should it come about to any appreciable degree, may prove to be a limited and temporary condition, but it is an interesting prospect, nonetheless.

Oceanic research—oceanography—is a relatively new area of scientific concern that is growing year by year, seeking to discover more about marine life, currents and tides, and many other secrets of the deep. Oil companies drill offshore with increasing frequency, hoping to find at least part of the answer to the serious energy shortage. It may be that there are many answers in and below the sea—including, perhaps, a few for which we do not as yet have questions.

To an Oyster

Cling fast
To the salt deep,
Answers in shells.
Your secrets,
Long ages kept,
Are too intimate
For us.
Our searchings
Are out to stars,
Our reachings
To distant voids.
There is only
The silence
Of mute laughter
From the craggy
Face of you.

Since the advent of extensive automotive travel, Maine has been noted as a recreational state, mostly in summer. Tourists from every other state and Canada partake of its beaches, boating, and fishing. Few visitors are fully aware of the state's seafaring past. The museum and old shipyard at Bath devoted to the shipbuilding days of sail is one of the very few available sources of Maine's maritime history. It would seem that more could be done to awaken, or renew, interest in the sailing ship era in Maine on the part of both private and public persons and organizations. As a tourist attraction another replica or two of early shipyards and sailing ships, along with ship museums and gift shops, could very well succeed in several coastal locations. No other state has a finer maritime background to recreate and display for its citizens and visitors alike, nor one more worthy of attention.

Waterfronts in coastal towns and cities all over the world have for many long centuries been places of particularly colorful and important activity. While the character of these waterfronts vary in differing degrees from one century to another and from country to country, the sea itself remains the constant factor—the ever-changing, never-changing sea.

Much of New England's history was enacted along its waterfronts, and many of them are hardly less active today. While ports no longer harbor large numbers of commercial ships, the volume of sea trade is far greater than ever. Freighters and tankers are huge, a single vessel carrying more than could have an entire fleet of sailing ships. Nor is there any comparison between the vast numbers of pleasure craft today—power or sail—and the relatively few such boats of only a generation or two ago.

Fishing trawlers, long past having to rely upon sail, continue to provide seafood, although often restricted in both fishing area and in catch limit due to many years of over fishing by outsized trawlers, usually of foreign origin and ownership.

Although inter-continental air travel has taken over most of the tourist business abroad, modern passenger ships—properly described as luxury cruisers—are still active to many vacation areas. Travel of all kinds has increased much faster than our population growth, which would seem to indicate, if not greater affluence, at least more interest in getting to know and understand people and places quite different from any we know even in this large and diversified country. Our curiosity, it appears, has not abated since the days of the western pioneers and the sailing ships.

* * * *

Where we are and where we are going is always of more immediate concern than the past, which is as it ought to be. Yet for sheer romance and a feeling of wonder akin to awe we inevitably harken back to the last century, to a time when life itself seemed somehow fresher and much less complicated. Certainly the glamor of the clippers and other sailing ships continues to arouse and excite us, even in these turbulent times. The reasons for their being or for their demise no longer matter in our daily lives. We view them from the standpoint of beauty and emotion, and find them to be unequalled on both counts. Odd as it may seem in this age of space exploration we still look backward to the sailing ships of the past with a depth of feeling far greater than that of mere nostalgia. Perhaps we are incurably romantic and more comfortable with what we know and understand. The vastness of outer space and the intricate and impersonal workings of our space program, while awesome to contemplate, seem too far removed from reality as we have known it. We still tend to think back to the achievements of the sea captains and other pioneers of old with nothing less than a feeling of envy. This despite the fact that we know full well that each generation must live in its own time and make the best of what it has or has not.

Whatever the wonders of this century and of those yet to come, the *Flying Cloud* and other equally beautiful clippers will always be the crowning glory of nineteenth century America.

And for me, personally, the *Scotland*, *Brandywine*, and the *Rising Sun* will surely sail forever like the ghost ships of their day, across the Atlantic and to ports in the Far East, totally immune to the ravages of storm and the encroachments of age and decay. While sailing ships were as mortal as is man himself, who can say that they were not possessed of a spirit as eternal as our own? If the hand and mind of man created them, and God created man—well, why not?

There is no need, of course, to resort to elaborating on the past or to indulge in overly sentimental musings. The facts are as clear as they are true, and do not require in depth detail to bring to immediate life. A tiny dot on the map such as Harpswell, Maine, can go unnoticed forever—as could have an even more remote Plains, Georgia. Only a person, or persons, can bring life to any place, however large or small. For a hundred years or more a few jagged miles of Maine coastline gave us ships and men fit to serve our growing land. In my time I merely report them. The beauty of truth is that it stands forever—recognized or not on its own merits.

* * * *

Before bringing our ship into port there are several loose ends to tie up. There is, for instance, the fact that we did not mention the great contributions of Searsport during the sailing era in Maine. This town produced more outstanding shipmasters per capita than any other along the entire Atlantic coast, and keeps its salty history alive today for the benefit of tourists in the area.

Nor did we once refer to Capt. Josiah Cressey, although the long time commander of the *Flying Cloud* was surely one of the best shipmasters of his time. (We will, however, resist the temptation to name other clipper captains, as this would only lead to further speculation as to their relative merits and abilities.)

And then there is the case of the *Flying Scud*. This very fast clipper, built in 1853 by the busy firm of Metcalf & Norris at Damariscotta, apparently made one remarkable run which, unfortunately, cannot be substantiated by logs. She was reported to have made 449 miles in one day, which would have been an all time record. In any case, the *Flying Scud* should be included in the "400 Club," whether or not such actual proof exists; and she made many other fine runs as well during her career.

Although we have now dropped anchor on our story of yesterday, today's horizons remain before us and are far wider than any envisioned in the days of sail. What is overwhelmingly important to us now are the courses we must set for them, today and in the future, and our ability to navigate inevitably stormy waters. Our voyage into the past is a tale complete and a part of our history as a people and as a nation. Whatever challenges may lie ahead, to our ship and to ourselves, we can surely meet with confidence. Given our proud heritage and our great resources, it could scarcely be otherwise. Nothing came easy for the sailing captains of old, nor does the world today offer any immediate prospects of smooth sailing. Yet how can we possibly doubt that we will conquer the vast and as yet uncharted seas that reach out before us?

Youngster

Blood is a child
Of the salt sea.
The flowing red
Has its own
Ebb and flood,
And has survived

Countless storms
And shall again.
Life will grow
Until the day
That all the seas
Run dry.